Canadian Scientists and Inventors

Biographies of people who made a difference

Harry Black

Pembroke Publishers Limited

© 1997 Pembroke Publishers Limited
538 Hood Road
Markham, Ontario L3R 3K9

Canadian Cataloguing in Publication Data

Black, Harry S.,
        Canadian scientists and inventors : biographies of people
 who made a difference

Includes bibliographical references and index.
ISBN 1-55138-081-1

1. Scientists — Canada — Biography.   2. Inventors — Canada —
Biography.   I.   Title.

Q141.B54 1997   509′.2′271   C97-931430-5

Editor: Cynthia Young
Design: John Zehethofer
Illustrations: Harry S. Black
Typesetting: JayTee Graphics

Printed and bound in Canada
9 8 7 6 5 4 3 2 1

Table of Contents

ACKNOWLEDGEMENTS

A book like this only looks uncomplicated when it is complete!

To accumulate sufficient information on some of these "significant" but often obscure Canadians required a great deal of sleuthing on my part and a lot of help from others.

Fortunately, there are repositories of information in Canada that keep Canadian history alive. First and foremost are the National Archives of Canada in Ottawa, which really does have its finger on Canada's past. The marvelous, "ancient" books and historical records that they maintain are of great value to Canada. Such materials would probably have been discarded almost anywhere else. I hope that the National Archives will always continue its important and valued work!

Second is the University of Toronto Archives, which does likewise. They also maintain a wonderful collection of notes, letters, correspondence, and newspaper clippings from the periods reviewed, and these materials shed a lucid light on the times, and humanize the historical.

I am deeply indebted to those who helped me personally to fill in the gaps in my own knowledge, to shed some light on Canada's past . . . and to keep the flame of Canadian history alive!

They include the following:

Harold Aberill, Archivist, and Barbara Edwards at University of Toronto; Laura Bradley, Archivist at Yarmouth County Museum and Historical Research Library; Evelyn M. Richardson of the Yarmouth County Museum Archives; Lyn Delgati, Archivist, National Research Council in Ottawa; Marc Ducharme, Registrar at the National Aviation Museum in Ottawa; Marina Englesakis, Director of Library Services at the Canadian Memorial Chiropractic College; Michael Lipowski of the Toronto Historical Board; The City of Toronto Archives and the Market Gallery of The City of Toronto Archives; George Murray and other members of the archives staff at the National Archives in Ottawa; Linda Scott of the Information Office of Imperial Oil Ltd. (for finding some "ancient" copies of the wonderful *Imperial Oil Review* newsmagazine); Judy Clubine of the Corporate Communications Department of Union Carbide.

A special word of thanks is reserved for Barbara Myrvoid, Toronto Public Library Archivist, for helping me to find the "unfindable"! And to Marie-Helene Sinquin, who typed and recorded this manuscript by reading the "unreadable."

A special word of thanks is also extended to Cynthia Young, the editor of this book, who has patiently absorbed my rantings about the integrity of words and the sacredness of ideas, and who has then gone patiently about the business of making my writing into a readable book.

To all of them, I extend my thanks.

Harry S. Black

Those Who Got Us Here!

Whether most Canadians recognize it or not, Canadian scientists and inventors have, in a quiet way, made exceptional contributions to our modern world. We see the results of their work all around us as we go about our daily lives, from the newspaper we read in the morning to the radio we listen to at night.

It could be said that all inventors have a touch of genius. But what is genius? The Oxford Dictionary says it is the possession of "a native intellectual power of an exalted type; an extraordinary capacity for imaginative creation, original thought, invention or discovery." That covers almost everyone in this book — from McIntosh, whose chance discovery gave us a new variety of apple to Polanyi, who developed the intellectually complex theory for the chemical laser.

It may be difficult to define genius, but it is not difficult to recognize its results.

A person of genius can conceptualize "things that never were," then create them, and make them work — often against the tide of conventional wisdom, as Fessenden did with his wave theory of sound transmission. But creating the invention was not the end of the process for most inventors. They faced many roadblocks along the way to recognition. The scientific establishment challenged Frederick Banting, Charles Best, and Harriet Brooks. In her male-dominated field, Brooks was also disadvantaged by her sex. Bell and Patch were blocked by the power of patent offices. Corporations challenged Gesner's and Patch's rights to their inventions and discoveries.

Then there are those at the other end of the spectrum, who have received powerful international recognition, like a Nobel Prize or a knighthood, for their accomplishments. The Nobel Prize for Science was established by Alfred Nobel, the Swedish inventor of dynamite, and is awarded each year to outstanding contributors in three branches of science: chemistry, physics, and medicine.[1] Five Canadian scientists have been recipients of the Nobel Prize for Science: Frederick Banting, Gerhard Herzberg, John MacLeod, John Polanyi, and Bertram N. Blockhouse. This book has profiles

---

[1] Lester B. Pearson, a former Prime Minister of Canada, was also a recipient of the Nobel Prize for Peace.

about three of these scientists. And there are probably several other Canadian scientists who should have received a Nobel Prize.[2] Six of the scientists in this book received knighthoods from the Crown of England, including Samuel Cunard, John McLennan, William Stephenson, Charles Saunders, Frederick Banting and Sandford Fleming.

We tend to think of all these inventors as occupying a separate space and time from each other, when in fact, many of them knew each other, and their lives overlapped in very human ways.

Thomas Edison gave both Reginald Fessenden and Rupert Turnbull their first real opportunity to exercise their brilliance by employing them in his New Jersey labs. The same Thomas Edison was a diabetic, who was one of the first beneficiaries of Frederick Banting's discovery of insulin. So too was King George V of Britain, who had previously pinned a medal on the 20-year-old Banting for his bravery in World War I. Samuel Cunard used the screw propeller invented by fellow Maritimer John Patch on his pioneering ocean liners that eventually revolutionized sea transportation. John Polanyi, the Nobel Prize winner who pioneered chemical laser technology, worked with Gerhard Herzberg, another Nobel Prize winner when they were both at the National Research Council in Ottawa and both were born in Germany.

Two of the inventors in this book were physics professors at the University of Toronto — Eli Franklin Burton and John C. McLennan. Reginald Fessenden and William Stephenson both retired to Bermuda and are better known there than they are in Canada. When George Desbarats moved from Ottawa, he sold his beautiful mansion to his friend Sir Sandford Fleming. J.J. Wright also exhibited his electric lighting system at the same Philadelphia Exposition that Alexander Graham Bell first successfully demonstrated his telephone. Donald Smith, who was the driving force behind the completion of the Canadian Pacific Railway was a benefactor to McGill University in Montreal and endowed the University with scholarships for bright young women to pursue their academic careers. These young women were known at the university as "Donaldas," and Harriet Brooks was one of them.

And finally a word about a special invention that was not the

---

[2] The essays about Reginald Fessenden, Charles Best, and Harriet Brooks clearly show that these individuals were deserving, but unrewarded in this regard.

creation of one person, but of 14,000. The story of the Avro *Arrow* is one of Canada's growing legends and a political story that just won't go away.

Created by the Canadian A.V. Roe aircraft industry at Malton, Ontario, in the early 1950s, the Avro *Arrow* looked like a dream and was probably the best fighter plane in the world at the time. It was a sleek, beautiful, delta-winged fighter aircraft that could fly at twice the speed of sound and had all the best technology that was then available. But the Avro *Arrow* had been enormously costly to produce, and there were no international purchasers on the horizon. That it existed at all was a matter of some national and political pride on the part of both the people of Canada and the Canadian government.

A landslide election victory in 1958 kept John Diefenbaker in power as the Prime Minister of Canada. Since the opposition party (the Liberals) held so few seats in the house, Diefenbaker had a great deal of political freedom. While many Canadians are not familiar with Diefenbaker's other accomplishments during his time as Prime Minister, most do know that Diefenbaker put an end to the Avro *Arrow* production plans soon after he was elected.

Production of the *Arrow* was stopped, closing down the plant and resulting in an immediate loss of 14,000 jobs at A.V. Roe. Most of the highly skilled designers and engineers drifted south to the United States, where they became key players in the American aircraft industry or at NASA (National Aeronautics and Space Administration). At the time, NASA was determined to send a person to the moon. In Canada, most of the political opposition and the former A.V. Roe employees hoped it would be John Diefenbaker!

Was the Avro *Arrow* the best fighter plane in the world? We may never know. The six prototype planes that had already been built were cut up and scrapped. Not even one complete *Arrow* was saved for display at the National Aviation Museum. This was seen by many as a vindictive act — that was unnecessary in the circumstances — not just the result of an economic issue.

Part of the mythology is that one prototype that crashed on a test run over Lake Ontario at Kingston lies at the bottom of the lake intact and, like King Arthur's sword *Excalibur*, it will one day be lifted from the Lake and shine once more as all legendary things do. In the meantime, the most the National Aviation Museum can display is a nose cone, a cockpit, and some beautiful photographs of a beautiful plane that is no more.

It is impossible for us to comprehend the world before any invention. But as you go about your daily routine, try to imagine a world without radio, T.V., photos in your newspaper, standard time, automobiles, airplanes, fax machines, electricity to power all your appliances, and all the other wonders of our modern world . . . and think of the people described in this book who gave them to us and got us here.

Frederick Banting and Charles Best

Medical Researchers: Discovery of Insulin

The first human patient treated with insulin was a 14-year-old boy with a severe case of juvenile diabetes. His recovery was remarkable and immediate.

Frederick Banting was born on November 19, 1891, on a farm near Alliston, Ontario. He attended school in Alliston, where he had an average but undistinguished academic career. He was an athletic, artistic, hard-working and determined student. In light of his average academic career, his later "discovery," arising from exceptional intellectual curiosity, brings into question the meaning of "genius" — which Banting surely was.

After graduating from high school, Banting entered Divinity College to satisfy his parents' wishes. He soon realized that medicine was his real interest, and he transferred into the medical program. When he graduated as a doctor in 1916, World War I was at its peak, and he felt compelled to do his part for his country. He enlisted in the Royal Canadian Army medical corps and was sent to Europe to work as a military surgeon in a rear field hospital. However, he was not satisfied and wanted to do more, so he transferred to the front at Cambrai, France. Under continuing enemy fire, the field medics treated the most severely wounded troops. Banting displayed great bravery in his field duties and was recommended for the King's Cross, which was not granted. He was later wounded by shrapnel, which severed an artery in his right arm. Even though his arm became badly infected, he refused to have it amputated because that would probably end his medical career. He was awarded the King's Cross this time, and the award was pinned on him personally by King George V.

After the war, he served for a year as resident surgeon at Toronto's Hospital for Sick Children. But for a young doctor just out of the army, earning a decent living was a practical necessity. So Banting opened a small practice in London, Ontario. He also lectured at the Medical School of the University of Western Ontario, and conducted research in neurophysiology under Dr. F. R. Miller.

One day while Banting was preparing a lecture on the pancreas, he read a paper by Moses Barron in a medical journal. The article described changes that occurred in the pancreatic juices when the pancreatic duct was blocked by gallstones. Banting was intrigued by the possibility that something that occurred in this process might hold the secret to diabetes — a disease that had distressed Banting since his schooldays, when a young classmate slowly wasted away from the disease before his eyes and finally died in her teens.

Diabetes was first recorded by Roman physicians almost 2,000 years ago. It is a debilitating disease that leaves its victims listless and suffering from progressive weight loss. The only treatment in 1920 was a strict diet that was generally incapable of sustaining a healthy body. Thus diabetes was often a death sentence for its victims.

The moment of genius for Banting came when he awoke from his sleep that night with the Barron article still on his mind. He wrote himself a note: "Tie off pancreas ducts of dogs. Wait six or eight weeks. Remove and extract."[1] It was generally known that the pancreas was the control centre for diabetes. Banting's focus was on the Islets of Langerhans, a part of the pancreas that clearly had a separate and distinct function of its own. He believed that

[1] Tyler Wasson, Editor. *Nobel Prize Winners* (An H.W. Wilson Biographical Dictionary; New York: H.W. Wilson Co., 1987), p. 520.

14

if the hormone secretion from the Islets of Langerhans could be isolated, it might be the control substance for diabetes.

He now had the idea, but he had neither a lab nor the funds for the necessary research. Miller advised Banting that Dr. John MacLeod of the University of Toronto had the facilities and that he might be interested in helping Banting. Banting arranged a meeting with MacLeod and took the long trip to Toronto to explain his proposal to him. MacLeod was not much impressed, and Banting went away empty-handed.

However, Banting's determination kept him focused on his goal. After additional research and with a more elaborate written proposal, he again met with MacLeod, who was somewhat more impressed this time. He told Banting that he would be in Scotland for the summer, and that Banting could have the use of a small lab, 10 dogs, and one of his assistants to work out his proposal in experimental form. Since Banting's medical practice in London was not large enough to keep him home, he immediately accepted MacLeod's offer. The assistant assigned to Banting was Charles Best, and thus was formed the team that unlocked the secrets of the pancreas and discovered "insulin," the hormone that became the successful treatment for diabetes.

Their experiments followed the line of Banting's inspired midnight note. By tying off the pancreatic ducts of several of the dogs for seven weeks, Banting and Best destroyed the other functions of the pancreas; however, the Islets of Langerhans continued to produce insulin. Banting and Best then extracted and injected the insulin into a diabetic dog. The dog recovered, and its blood sugar level returned to normal. Their experiment had succeeded, and Banting's assumptions were proven correct.

When MacLeod returned, he was suitably impressed that the breakthrough had been made and that the discovery of insulin would lead to the successful treatment of diabetes. But much experimental work still had to be done, the processes refined, and the substance purified to make it safe for human use. MacLeod put the full resources of his department at Banting's disposal. Among the "resources" were the services of J. B. Collip, a skilled biochemist, who refined and purified the insulin product.

The first human patient treated with insulin was a 14-year-old boy with severe juvenile diabetes. His recovery was remarkable and immediate. Other patients followed, with the same impressive results.

When the discovery of insulin was announced to the world, there was considerable confusion over who had actually discovered it. This happened partly because MacLeod, who was a highly respected doctor and researcher, referred to the discovery in a way that implied that it was his and that Banting and Best were his assistants.

This misunderstanding was reinforced by media reports in the United States and Europe that attributed the discovery to MacLeod. Banting was justifiably furious over this unnecessary confusion. Finally, after nine months of silence, MacLeod made a public statement clearly attributing the idea to Banting and the discovery to Banting and Best — with valued assistance from MacLeod's physiology department at the University of Toronto.

Obviously, the product would not have been available to the world so quickly without the recognition of its importance by MacLeod and without the help that his department provided to Banting and Best. But the discovery was theirs, and theirs alone.

For Banting, the discovery of insulin meant sudden fame, and he was soon showered with honours. Diabetics from all over the world came to Toronto for treatment. Every patient, including the rich and famous, wanted to meet him. Among the many early recipients of insulin were Thomas Edison, H. G. Welles, and King George V.

A grateful Canadian government granted Banting a lifetime annuity. In 1923, he and MacLeod received the Nobel prize for Medicine. But Banting was again incensed that Charles Best was not included in the honour. Members of the Nobel Committee later admitted privately that Best should have been awarded a share of the prize.

Banting gave half his prize to Charles Best, and the other half to the Banting Medical Research Foundation. In addition, Banting did not personally patent his discovery, although it would have made him very wealthy. Instead, he turned over his rights to the University of Toronto, which passed the rights for manufacturing insulin to the Medical Research Council of Canada. Banting's gestures were a measure of the man. In 1934, he was knighted by King George V, and from that point on, although he could use the title "Sir" Frederick Banting, he preferred to be called Doctor or "Chief."

In 1930, the Banting Institute was opened at the University of Toronto, and Banting's new department of medical research was housed there. In addition to improving the quality and quantity of insulin, his team carried out research in many other health-related fields, including cancer, lead poisoning in children, silicosis in miners, and polio treatment.

When World War II started in 1939, Banting became chairman of the National Research Council's Committee on Aviation Medical Research. This was a new field of research since planes could now fly higher, faster, and farther than ever before. Through this work, he became directly involved with the British Air Ministry, and in the fall of 1939, he went to Britain. Banting also volunteered to serve as a liaison officer with the RCAF (Royal Canadian Air Force) to convey important messages to Britain.

In early 1941, under a cloak of secrecy, he again set out for Britain to discuss his research with his British colleagues. His plane took off from Newfoundland on February 21, but soon developed engine trouble and turned back. It crashed in an isolated area only 15 minutes flying time from the airport, killing all three passengers, including Frederick Banting. Only the pilot survived to tell of the events before the crash that killed one of Canada's most respected and revered sons.

Alexander Graham Bell

Inventor: Telephone, Communication Devices, and Transportation Technologies

He thought he could harness the new electronic technology by creating a machine with a transmitter and receiver that would send sounds telegraphically to help deaf people hear.

Was he a Scot, a Canadian, or an American? Well . . . he was all three at one point or another in his lifetime, so it is not surprising that Scotland, Canada, and the United States *all* claim him as their own. I recently read a book about famous Scots, which not only included him in its pages, but had his portrait on the cover! Another book, about American inventors, lists him as one of the most famous. A sign on the outskirts of Brantford, Ontario proudly proclaims the city as the place where the telephone was invented by the famous Canadian Brantford-resident: Alexander Graham Bell.

By Bell's own account, his Canadian links are firmly established. He himself acknowledged that research on the telephone was carried out in Brantford in the summer of 1874, and the first practical long distance call was made on August 10, 1876, between Brantford and Paris, Ontario. Bell's other major innovation, the

18

hydrofoil, was invented, developed, and tested at his retirement home in Baddeck, Nova Scotia.

However, he was born in Scotland, educated at the University of Edinburgh and the University of London, and when he was 23 years old, he emigrated with his family to Canada and settled in Brantford, Ontario. Two of Alexander's brothers had died of tuberculosis, and his parents believed their deaths were partly due to the Scottish climate. Alexander began to show some of the same pulmonary weaknesses as his brothers. Not wanting to risk the life of their son, the Bells moved to Canada, where Alexander's father could continue to practise his profession as a speech therapist to the deaf.

Bell's father and grandfather were both elocution teachers. His father also wrote *The Standard Elocutionist*, the definitive training manual on the subject, and it has gone through 200 editions. His father also developed a lip reading system for the deaf, which he called "visible speech."

Alexander followed in his father's and grandfather's footsteps, teaching and working with the deaf. As his father's assistant, he sought to improve upon the visible speech system by using electrical sound enhancement. He thought he could harness the new electronic technology by creating a machine with a transmitter and receiver that would send sounds telegraphically to help deaf people hear. This led to his broadening interest in distance telegraphic sound transmission. He carried out his experiments in both his family home in Brantford, and in his new home in Boston, Massachusetts, where, by 1874, he was the vocal physiology professor at Boston University.

It is often true in the world of invention that work on the same invention is going on simultaneously in several places. Bell had been seeking a U.S. patent for some time and it was granted only days before several of his competitors also applied for patents on similar machines. In his patent submission, he described his device as "the method of, and apparatus for, transmitting vocal or other sounds telegraphically ... by causing electrical undulations similar in form to the vibrations of the air accompanying the said vocal or other sounds." He was subsequently forced to defend the ownership of his invention in court and was successful.

His "telephone," as he called the invention, was the sensation of the Centennial Exhibition in Philadelphia, Pennsylvania, in

1876; however, it had gained little attention in the early days of the Exhibition until the Emperor of Brazil visited his display with an entourage of journalists in tow. The Emperor was so taken with Bell's "telephone" after a personal demonstration by Bell that his enthusiasm was reflected in the reports that appeared in the newspapers the following day. Bell became famous almost instantly, and the telephone was put to practical use almost immediately. In 1877, Bell was the key player in setting up the company that still bears his name today. The telephone also made him very wealthy, which allowed him to do what he loved best: teach and invent.

While he is famous throughout the world today for inventing the telephone, he is also credited with many other important discoveries that have had a significant impact on twentieth century society! Among them is the hydrofoil, which is used worldwide today in "ferry boat" service. This high-speed water craft travels above the water on metal projecting foils. Bell's full-scale prototype hydrofoil was tested near his home at Baddeck, Nova Scotia, in 1917, and it was able to reach speeds of over 100 kilometres an hour. It was the fastest boat in the world at the time.

He also took a special interest in "flying machines" and established the Aerial Experiment Association in 1907. It was a small group of bright, dedicated young people, including Alex Baldwin, John McCurdy, and Glenn Curtiss. With Bell, they designed, built, and flew a variety of motor-powered aircraft, including the *Silver Dart*. It was the first Canadian-built plane to fly in Canada and was piloted by Canadian John McCurdy, who later became Lieutenant Governor of Nova Scotia.

Many of us have sat idly looking out the window of an airliner, fascinated by the small hinged section at the rear of the wings that moves up and down in flight. It provides in-flight stability to the plane and makes minor flight corrections. Called an aileron, this indispensable element of a modern airplane was also Bell's invention, as was the tricycle wheel landing gear that replaced the landing skis on earlier planes. A more sophisticated version of the tricycle landing gear is still used on airplanes today.

Bell also invented a wax recording cylinder for his phonograph machine, a prototype iron lung, and several gadgets for the enhancement of hearing. In all, Bell is credited with over 100 inventions, most of which were related to sound or flight, and all together, made him one of the world's most prolific inventors.

If that was not enough for a busy life, he was also co-founder of the *National Geographic Magazine,* and served as the president of the National Geographic Society from 1896 to 1904.

The Bell Homestead in Brantford is now the Bell Telephone Museum, which commemorates Bell's invention of the telephone. The National Aviation Museum in Ottawa recognizes his contribution to flying in a prominent display of his work, including a full-scale model of the *Silver Dart.* His home in Baddeck, where he spent the last 36 years of his life, is also a museum that displays many of his original inventions.

The monument in front of the Bell Homestead, which was unveiled by Queen Elizabeth II on June 28, 1997, states:

"Here at his parents' home in July 1874, Alexander Graham Bell conceived the fundamental idea of the telephone and in August 1876 carried out the first long distance trials."

He retained a lifelong dedication to the improvement of communication systems for the congenitally deaf. His wife Mabel Hubbard was deaf and had been one of Bell's pupils. Helen Keller was another of Bell's pupils and dedicated her autobiography to him. Asked late in life what his greatest accomplishment had been, Bell said it was his work with the deaf.

Bell loved his work with airplanes and had a lifelong passion for teaching the deaf. However, he never had much affection for his most famous invention. "I never use the beast," he said of his own telephone, whose bell he stuffed with paper.[1]

While most of us could not live without our various telephones, there are few of us who would not echo these same sentiments at times!

[1] Carole P. Shaw. *Famous Scots* (Glasgow: Harper Collins Publishing, 1995), p. 19.

Armand Bombardier

Inventor: The Snowmobile

This wild and dangerous machine apparently worked, and making it work better became the lifelong passion of Armand.

Armand Bombardier was born in Valcourt, Quebec, in 1907. By the time he was 15 years old, he was already demonstrating the mechanical skills that would one day make him both rich and famous. To give him tangible experience, his father gave him an old car and a garage to work in. Armand turned the car into his first tentative snowmobile, and the garage into a thriving automobile repair business. To make his first primitive snowmobile, he removed the engine from the old car, repaired it, and then mounted it on the back of a platform that had skis on it. He replaced the radiator fan with a home-made propeller, which he pointed backwards. This wild and dangerous machine apparently worked, and making it work better became the lifelong passion of Armand.

While he developed his own business, Armand Bombardier continued to tinker with designs for a snowmobile. In 1934, his young son died from appendicitis because a raging snowstorm prevented Armand from getting to the hospital in time to save him. Only a snow vehicle might have saved his son's life and could undoubtedly serve in other emergencies as well. He began in earnest to adapt his design from all the best ideas that had come to him. In 1935, he designed a rubber-covered track and drive wheel, and placed it at the rear of a vehicle, with skis mounted on the front to steer it. It was the first successful rear track drive snowmobile, which is the standard design in use today. With this prototype vehicle that looked like the cars of the time, Bombardier travelled throughout the province of Quebec, promoting his invention. It was a hit with the public and the media alike. The two secrets to its success were the soft tank-like tread at the rear (which held up in snow like a snowshoe) and the simple crawl mechanism that drove the tracks.

In 1937, he patented his invention as B.7 (for Bombardier, seven-passenger snow vehicle) and he manufactured and sold 50 of them, mainly for buses, ambulances, police, and emergency use. It was not a recreation vehicle — yet!

During World War II, he made a modified version for military use, and a larger 12-passenger version like a bus, for carrying passengers in snowy places like the mountains, ski resorts, and other populated areas with large quantities of snow.

He continued to fiddle with the design to improve its function, but the vehicle's bulky size never appealed to a large audience. Not until the 1950s, with the introduction of the small but powerful air cooled engines, was he able to scale down his snowmobile to the size of a motorcycle. And then the world changed! He called his first small-scale snowmobile the "ski dog," but changed it to "Ski Doo," the name that is now synonymous with the vehicle.

He had created a phenomenon! It was so successful that production could not keep up with orders. Bombardier's Ski Doo soon faced numerous competitors who imitated Bombardier's design. At one point, there were over 50 manufacturers around the world, all producing similar snowmobiles. In the 1960s, there were over 250,000 snowmobiles sold annually in the North American market, and Bombardier was producing half of them.

Why the phenomenal success? What had once been inaccessible now became accessible. What had been too expensive, was now within reach of almost everyone. And Ski Doos were fun to ride! More importantly, they changed the face of winter recreation and transportation forever! They provided a way to travel easily, efficiently, and rapidly over vast stretches of snow-covered land in relative comfort and safety — an important feature for anyone who needed or wanted to travel in winter.

After Armand Bombardier's death in 1964, the company diversified more broadly into the field of transportation, including aircraft, trains, subway cars, and the Sea Doo (a Ski Doo for water sport).

When I was in Bangkok several years ago, people there told me that their new subway system was being considered by Bombardier of Canada. It is a long way to Bangkok from a small garage in Valcourt, Quebec.

Dr. Roberta Bondar

Research Scientist: Astronaut, Doctor, and Neurobiologist

Everything she did from the time she was a child, she did with one goal firmly in mind: to become an astronaut!

Roberta Bondar looks like an astronaut should: strong, self-assured, athletic, supremely confident, and attractive. When she speaks, she is articulate, forceful, and knowledgeable about her work and clear about her goals. If there seems to be an edge in what she says, you feel she has a very good reason for saying it that way. She looks as if she has been groomed for this role all her life . . . And she has been groomed! By herself.

Everything she did — from the time she was a child who dreamed of flying in outer space, who built model rocket ships, and who played at being a super hero — she did with one goal firmly in mind: to become an astronaut!

She was nurtured in this dream by her parents, was encouraged by her aunt who worked for NASA, and was supported by the people around her whom she cared about. When she first dreamed of becoming an astronaut, the American space program had not really started. But the Russian space program had!

In 1961, the Russians jolted the world — and in particular, the

American government — with the orbital flight of Yuri Gagarin. He became the world's first astronaut and his flight launched the great age of space science that is still in its infancy. In the short time between that first flight and Roberta Bondar's flight in 1992, many exceptional milestones have been achieved, and we have learned vastly more about our universe than we could have thought possible in such a short period of time. (It took longer to build the pyramids!)

The first person to reach the surface of the moon was Neil Armstrong, who arrived there on the Apollo 11 rocket in 1969. Unpiloted space probes have landed on Mars and Venus and ventured past almost all the planets except Uranus and Pluto. They have sent back marvelous photos from space, including some of the planets' larger moons, the rings of Saturn, the red spot of Jupiter, and the asteroid belt. Canada contributed to space technology even before we had astronauts. Several of the space-launched television satellites that transmit signals around the world were put in orbit with the hi-tech, Canadian-made, robotic "Canadarm."

And in 1992, Roberta Bondar became a part of all that, just as she wanted to be.

Roberta Bondar was born in 1945 in Sault Ste Marie, Ontario. From her earliest recollections she always believed she was "part of the team." When the Apollo capsule circled the moon, Roberta imagined herself cramped in alongside the astronauts, and she shared in the triumphs and trials of all those who had gone before her.

Everything she did — from her formal education to flying lessons — was part of her plan to fulfill her dream and become an astronaut. She was also realistic enough to know that she was working against tremendous odds. All the astronauts in the first two decades of the program had been jet fighter pilots from either Russia or the United States, because those countries owned all the rockets. And all the astronauts had been men.

Roberta learned to fly when she was in her teens. However, in high school, she came up against another barrier when she was advised to take courses other than math or science. She not only took science in high school, but earned four university science degrees: a Bachelor's Degree in Zoology from the University of Guelph, a Master of Pathology Degree from the University of Western Ontario, a Ph.D. in Neurobiology from the University of Toronto, and a Medical Degree from McMaster University in Hamilton.

Once she was qualified as a medical doctor, she accepted a position as assistant professor in neurobiology at McMaster, and got on with her life. However, she believed (quite rightly) that scientists, medical doctors, and other specialists would eventually be included in the astronaut selection process because space exploration would require a great deal more knowledge and more diversified skills than could be provided by jet fighter pilots alone.

In July 1983, the National Research Council in Ottawa established a Canadian Astronaut Program to find candidates to fly in the American Space Shuttle. They put an ad in newspapers across the country appealing for candidates to be part of a scientific team that would be sent into space. (Yes! They placed an ad in the newspaper.) And there appeared to be no special restrictions for qualified candidates! It would be a matter of selecting the very best from among those who responded. And 4,300 people did, including Roberta Bondar.

Through the process of elimination the selection committee had narrowed the field down to 19 candidates by November 1983. Roberta was one of them . . . but was the only woman! By December 4, 1983, when the final selection was made, there were only six candidates. And Roberta was still one of them! When she got the call, it meant the end of her independent life and the beginning of an intensive training period that would continue for most of the next decade.

But in 1986, tragedy struck suddenly. The *Challenger* shuttle blew up spectacularly shortly after launch, killing all seven astronauts on board and casting a pall of uncertainty over the future of the "shuttle" program. Everything was put on hold while the U.S. government reassessed its plans. Changes had to be made to improve the safety of future missions and NASA had the problem of trying to placate and reassure a shaken government. Would the money dry up and the program be scrapped? After several years, the program was eventually restarted, and Roberta was told that she (or fellow Canadian-astronaut candidate Ken Money) would fly on a future shuttle mission. Her intensive training began once again. This time the issue of her being a woman began to surface in the media. She put the issue to rest publicly by stating that it was a "catch-22" for her. "There were those who would say that if she was not chosen it was because she was a woman and there would be those who would say that if she was chosen it was because she was a woman. The reality is that she had the qualifications." And NASA agreed! Even her fellow candidates agreed publicly that she had the "Right Stuff." It was a job she had prepared for all her life.

On January 22, 1992, four astronauts, including Dr. Roberta Bondar, boarded the space shuttle *Discovery* at Cape Canaveral, Florida. The moment she had lived for all her life had arrived. Time stood suspended for them as they waited in limbo, strapped in their seats, while the launch was delayed for almost an hour because of weather. And then . . . She was off on the adventure of her life, beginning with two minutes of incredibly violent vibrations.

"As payload specialist, she worked at least 14 hour days and conducted some 55 scientific experiments."[1] Her role, as a doctor and a neurobiologist, was to study the effect of weightlessness on the human body. After her return to Earth, she continued in this role with NASA, where she served as an advisor, a mentor, and a role model for younger and less experienced scientists in the space program.

While she continues to work with NASA, she has dropped out of the Canadian space program and returned to McMaster University. What her future will bring is difficult even for her to say. Most likely, she will continue to teach and conduct research at a university where she can use her knowledge, education, and experience to work with new generations of young people. Wherever her research takes her, the sky is not necessarily the limit.

While all the scientists and inventors in this book should be famous, for the most part they are not. Roberta Bondar is one of the exceptions. There are few Canadians, if any, who do not know who Roberta Bondar is or what she has done. Most would know that she was an astronaut, a space pioneer, and an adventurer. She is an admirable role model; someone almost larger-than-life because she has done something that most of us dream of, but that few of us will ever do. Would she see herself in these terms? She would probably describe herself more realistically: as a doctor and a scientist who had the good fortune to be on the front end of humanity's next great adventure — the exploration of outer space. And as she said, "Once an astronaut, always an astronaut."

[1] John Colapinto, "Woman of the Year," *Chatelaine*, January 1993, p. 63.

Harriet Brooks

Research Scientist and Pioneer: Radioactivity and Co-discoverer of Radon

By giving the new substance an atomic weight — something which only elements have — was Brooks not also saying that the substance was a new element?

Harriet Brooks was a pioneer nuclear physicist at the turn of the twentieth century when nuclear physics was still considered a "new" science. Among her significant contributions to the field were her co-identification of the element now known as radon; the radical theory that one element could turn into another during the radioactive decay process; and her foundation work for what later became known as the "recoil theory" of atoms. All three contributions are building blocks to our understanding of radioactivity.

Harriet Brooks was born into a relatively poor family in Exeter, Ontario, in 1876. After many moves, the Brooks family settled in Montreal, Quebec. Harriet was a brilliant student, and through scholarships, she was able to attend McGill University — only six years after women there were granted degrees and only twelve years after they were granted anywhere in Canada. One of her scholarships had been donated by Lord Strathcona (Donald

Smith), the same Donald Smith who built the Canadian Pacific Railway and drove in the last spike.

In Brooks' day, the attitude about women attending university was very strange. Astonishingly, a famous doctor could suggest that "higher education for women . . . was unhealthy and could jeopardize their child bearing potential." But even more astonishing, this view was shared by many!

She graduated from McGill with highest honours and joined Ernest Rutherford at McGill University's McDonald Laboratory as his first graduate student. Rutherford had been lured away from the Cavendish Lab in Cambridge to the superior modern facility at McGill, and it was Brooks' good fortune to work with him while he was there. They became and remained close friends throughout their lives.

At the time, work on nuclear physics was pure research. Very little was known about radioactivity; even less about the deadly properties of radioactive substances like radium, thorium, polonium, and radon; and nothing about the radioactive decay process itself.

In his experiments, Rutherford had detected that radioactive substances like radium gave off "something" that was like a gas but was not a gas. He called this substance an "emanation." He gave Harriet Brooks the responsibility of identifying this substance and the processes it was going through. She and her team determined that it appeared to be a new substance that was not radium, and that it had an identifiable atomic weight. By giving the new substance an atomic weight — something which only elements have — was Brooks not also saying that the substance was a *new element*? This discovery did two things. It identified the first step in the radioactive decay process and it led to the identification of a new element that was eventually named radon. But it did something else! It challenged the long-held theory that changing one element into another was not possible (unless you were an alchemist or Merlin the magician).

Rutherford and Brooks presented a joint paper on their discovery to the Royal Society of Canada titled "The New Gas from Radium." Rutherford published another article under his own name in *Nature* magazine in which he credited Brooks' assistance. The scientific community was, and is, slow to recognize anything new and unproven, until it has the endorsement of an established scientist — which Rutherford was, but Brooks was not! If the discovery had been put forward under her name, the paper would likely have been ignored by the scientific community — as later proved to be the case when she submitted her paper on the "recoil theory" of atoms.

In 1901, she accepted a graduate fellowship in physics at Bryn Mawr, a women's college in Pennsylvania that catered to brilliant students and was dedicated to scholarly excellence. At Bryn Mawr, Brooks was awarded the prestigious European Fellowship that was given to "the most able graduate student." This award gave her the opportunity to attend any European university of her choice for one year. Harriet chose Cambridge, where she worked at the Cavendish Lab with J.J. Thomson, another noted pioneer nuclear physicist.

It was not the most rewarding or stimulating period in her life, except perhaps at tea time, when she was "allowed" to serve tea with the other women. She found Thomson unhelpful to her, and it was probably during this year that she decided not to pursue a career in physics. However, she returned to the McDonald Lab at McGill and continued her work with Rutherford.

In her further study of radioactive particles through the decay process of radium, she noted that the particles were ejected in all directions, and some were deposited on the sides of the container, while the rest dispersed in the air. This indicated that a volatile activity, which she termed "an invisible radioactive snowstorm,"[1] was taking place. The invisible snowstorm she had observed was fully reported on by Rutherford at his Bakerian Lecture in London in 1904. But it was not generally accepted by the scientific community at the time. The term "recoil theory" was coined by Harriet's brother-in-law, who was a professor of physics at McGill. Perhaps Brooks should have used the term first.

Four years later in 1908, Otto Hahn, a German physicist who had worked with Rutherford at McGill, "rediscovered the phenomenon,"[2] but this time, it was generally accepted! Rutherford wrote to him, "by the way, I thought I had reported on the removal

[1] Maralene F. Rayner-Canham and Geoffrey W. Rayner-Canham. *Harriet Brooks: Pioneer Nuclear Physicist* (Montreal/Kingston: McGill-Queen's University Press, 1992), p. 40.
[2] Rayner and Rayner, p. 41.

of atoms by recoil in my book on page _. It is given in an explanation of the volatility of radium observed by Miss Brooks."[3] Hahn noted that he was unfamiliar with Brooks' work, but her observations were not those of the recoil phenomena."[4] However, Rutherford thought they were.

After an abortive year teaching physics at Bernard College, Brooks met Maxim Gorky, the famous Russian revolutionary writer, and Maria Andeyeva, at an Adirondacks resort in New York. She travelled to Italy with them and spent the fall on the Isle of Capri at their villa. This part of her life came to light in the papers of Gorky and not in the Canadian historical records.

During her exciting but relatively short career as a nuclear physicist, she worked with Marie Curie in 1906 and 1907, and her name appears in some of Curie's technical papers.

When Harriet Brooks married the prevailing attitude at most universities was that marriage and science did not mix — unless you were a man. The system discouraged her and many young women. She eventually drifted out of active research. While she was central to much of the early pioneering work in nuclear physics, her name appeared only as an associate on someone else's work — because that is how it was done. Her original work put forward in her own papers was ignored officially at the time or was "rediscovered" by others.

She died in 1933 of "radiation-related illnesses." Many of the early scientists in this field had similar illnesses because the deadly properties of radioactive substances were not known, and scientists worked unprotected with these dangerous materials. When Rutherford and Curie's papers were re-opened many years later, they were still radioactive. Brooks' death followed a series of personal tragedies, including the death of her 20-year-old daughter, who was found drowned in the St. Lawrence River in mysterious circumstances.

In the obituary he wrote about Brooks for *Nature*, Rutherford gave her full credit for the significant contribution she had made to the "then youthful science of radioactivity." He said that

---

[3] Rayner and Rayner, p. 41.
[4] Rayner and Rayner, p. 41.

"next to Madame Curie, Brooks was the most outstanding woman in the field of radioactivity. He credited her identification of emanation (radon) as a vital piece of work that had led him to propose the theory of the transmutation of one element into another. This was a revolutionary view for a time when the unchangeability of atoms was a basic part of the then current scientific dogma. A subsequent piece of her research led to the idea of the successive changes of elements which was a key step to disentangling the complexities of radioactive decay. Finally, there was the discovery of the recoil of the radioactive atom, the item that has been most associated with her name."[5]

It is regrettable that more of his colleagues had not accorded her the same recognition for her pioneering work. But how different are we today? I could not find Harriet Brooks in any Canadian textbook, despite the considerable significance of her work. Why was she not recognized? The discoveries she made and reported in association with Rutherford received endorsement, but were generally attributed to the more famous scientist despite his full acknowledgment of Brooks' contribution! On the other hand, the works she published alone were ahead of conventional wisdom of the scientific community, and the framework for accepting a radical new theory was not there. In addition, because she was a young researcher, her ideas could be more easily ignored or discounted.

Of particular interest is that she is the only physicist known to have worked with all three of the great nuclear physicists: Ernest Rutherford, J.J. Thomson, and Marie Curie. It is also interesting to note that all three were awarded Nobel Prizes for work that Brooks contributed to directly. And for the sake of neatness, it would have been "nice" to have given her one too!

[5] Rayner and Rayner, p. 105.

Dr. Eli Franklin Burton

Inventor: The Electron Microscope

Overall, the great advantages that the electron microscope offered to science and industry were its vast improvement in magnification, its clarity of detail, and its revelation of things that could not be seen before.

When Galileo first looked at the heavens through his simple telescope in 1609, it was the beginning of humankind's voyage of discovery through vast and limitless space — the universe beyond our world. The same principle of Galileo's telescope was adapted by the Dutch inventor Anton van Leeuwenhoek who in 1674 turned his lenses inward on the miniature world of insects, germs, microbes, and cells. In so doing, van Leeuwenhoek started another voyage of discovery . . . to the world of the infinitely small. "The universe in a drop of water!"[1]

Telescopes and microscopes both operate on the same principle of magnification. Objects are viewed through optical lenses that are combined to enlarge the image . . . of a planet . . . or an insect. The standard optical microscope relies on the use of light rays. Its magnification is limited by the wavelength of the light that it uses.

[1] *Imperial Oil Review*, February 1946.

It cannot produce an image of objects that are closer together than the length of a light wave. But the invention of the electron microscope changed all that!

Electrons are about two million times smaller than light waves, and the effective wavelength of speeding electrons is infinitely smaller compared to that of light waves. Thus, the effective wavelength of speeding electrons can produce images of objects so small that 10 million of them side by side would be no longer than one centimetre. In addition, the images created by the electron microscope are so clear and crisp in detail that they retain their clarity even when photographically enlarged up to 50,000 times the size of the original object.

The electron microscope made it possible for scientists to see objects that had appeared only as "fuzzy shadows" through the standard optical microscope. Astonishingly, the electron microscope also revealed other objects so infinitely small that they had previously not been seen at all! For the first time, scientists could see viruses, which they had long suspected were the causes of illnesses such as "flu" or the common cold. They could see the active bodies in vaccines and serums that attack and kill germs. They could actually observe the effects of penicillin and other wonder drugs on bacteria. The electron microscope has also aided in the fight against cancer. It has opened up new vistas to scientists in genetic research by making it possible to see the genes and chromosomes that carry the hereditary factors in sex cells.

The electron microscope has also proven to be invaluable to industry in revealing the structure and composition of substances such as wood fibre, asphalt, textiles, plastics, paints, inks, dyes, paper coatings, metal surfaces, and photographic development processes, and in an infinite variety of other ways.

Overall, the great advantages that the electron microscope offered to science and industry were its vast improvement in magnification, its clarity of detail, and its revelation of things that could not be seen before.

The first practical electron microscope was the creation of Dr. Eli Franklin Burton and his team of scientists at the physics laboratory at the University of Toronto. His two colleagues were graduate students James Hillier and Albert Prebus. Other scientists — including Dr. Ernst Ruska, whom Burton had visited at his laboratory in Berlin in 1935 — had been working along similar lines.

However, it was Burton who first constructed a practical and successful electron microscope, which he tested in 1938.

In the test, Burton and his colleagues viewed a razor blade through an optical microscope, and it still looked like a razor blade. But when viewed through the electron microscope, the same razor blade appeared to be a jagged mountain range of rugged peaks and valleys.

The electron microscope took us one step further in revealing the infinite, by helping to unlock the mysteries of the "invisible" universe around us. Dr. Burton would not have believed that his electron microscope would be considered his most important contributions to the world.

Eli Franklin Burton was born in 1879 at Green River, Ontario, just east of Toronto. He did his undergraduate degree at the University of Toronto. He earned his Masters Degree on a scholarship to Cambridge University. He then returned to the University of Toronto, where he received his Ph.D. in 1910. He was made associate professor in 1911, and full professor in 1924.

At the University of Toronto, Burton worked with Dr. J.C. McLennan (who was then director of the physics department) in finding and then liquefying helium. In 1932, he succeeded McLennan as the director of the physics department, and was also appointed director of the McLennan Physics Laboratory, which was named after his old friend and colleague. The new physics wing at the University of Toronto was eventually named the Burton Wing in recognition of Burton's own brilliance as a scientist, a teacher, and an inventor.

Burton had a great sense of flair and showmanship. He was particularly remembered at the University of Toronto for concluding one of his lectures on fibres by playing "'God Save the King' by dropping pieces of wood on his desk tuned to the notes on the scale."[2]

Burton was a great believer in demystifying science in order to make it understandable to the average person. He was often called on to give simplified explanations of the most complex subjects, such as the atomic bomb or the electron microscope. He was also a noted international speaker, and was invited to give lectures at

[2] From the obituary of Eli Franklin Burton, *The Toronto Star*, July 7, 1948.

many of the great universities and teaching institutions in North America, such as Harvard and the Mayo Clinic.

In addition, Burton conducted research on colloids (particles in suspension) to develop a treatment for cancer. He was an expert on cosmic rays and undertook special assignments to help the allies in World War II. He understood the importance of radar to the war effort and trained radar operators for the armed forces. As well, he was director of Research Enterprises Ltd. in Leaside, Ontario, which produced radar and other electronic equipment for the military.

Burton was awarded an Order of the British Empire in 1943 for his exceptional service to his country and his profession, and for expanding our knowledge of the world of "the infinitely small."

Samuel Cunard

Pioneer and Entrepreneur: Commercial Transatlantic Steamship Travel

The Cunard ocean liners set the standard for luxury and taste, as well as for speed, safety, and comfort at sea, epitomizing the passenger side of Britain's domination of the sea for over 100 years.

When I was a boy, the very name Cunard conjured up images of great adventure, of far exotic places across the sea, and of the great luxurious ships that plied the Atlantic Ocean, carrying the rich and famous of the day. These majestic ocean liners of my youth — the *Queen Mary*, the *Queen Elizabeth*, and the *Queen Elizabeth II* — were the last great ships of the legendary Cunard Steamship Company, which dominated the world of passenger travel before the age of the jumbo jet airliner. The great ships of the Cunard line set the standard for luxury and taste, as well as for speed, safety, and comfort at sea, epitomizing the passenger side of Britain's domination of the sea for over 100 years.

But if you go back about 200 years, you will find that Samuel Cunard, the founder of the Great British Steamship Line, was born in Halifax, Nova Scotia, in 1787. His parents, Abraham and Margaret Cunard, arrived in Halifax in 1780, after the American War of Independence, seeking sanctuary as United Empire Loyalists.

Abraham Cunard was a successful ship owner in the United States, but during the war, he remained loyal to Britain, and his business did not support the American cause. So, at the end of the war, he was stripped of his possessions, including his fleet of ships. With no future in the new United States of America, the Cunards, like thousands of others, made their way to Nova Scotia, one of the few remaining British colonies in North America.

They settled in the seaport of Halifax, which had become the major port of entry into British North America after the American War of Independence. As a United Empire Loyalist, Cunard was given a grant of land to start a new life. He wisely chose a site along the harbour. He had the skills of a shipwright and fortunately found a position as a carpenter on the docks of Halifax.

Halifax continued to grow and became a major world seaport. A large British garrison was stationed there, with a British Prince as the Commander in Chief. Halifax attracted many businesses because of its new and unique position in the British Empire.

It was a boom time in Halifax, which continued until the War of 1812 concluded, settling the remaining differences between Britain and the United States of America. The end of the War of 1812 also brought peace, which meant that Halifax no longer needed a major military garrison to protect the colonies. The position of major port of entry into North America shifted from Halifax to Boston and New York. Halifax was still important, but less so, and many businesses built during war, failed in peace.

By this time, Abraham Cunard had re-established his shipping interests through a diversified portfolio of trades, including ship repairs, ship building, ship outfitting, lumbering, and whaling. He became an enormously successful entrepreneur!

In 1787, his son Samuel was born, and he was brought up with his focus fixed firmly on the sea. In 1808, Abraham Cunard bought his first ship, which he named after his wife, Margaret. Under the ship's name he had added *A. Cunard and Son*, thus starting one of the world's great shipping lines. In this modest beginning, his first ship carried mainly products (not people) to ports along the east coast of North America.

Soon the Cunards added another ship, the *Nancy*, and then another, a handsome, sea-going square rigger sailing ship called the *White Oak*. In addition to shipping products, the *White Oak* was the first of the Cunard ships to carry passengers across the Atlantic.

In 1814, the year the war between the United States and Britain ended, Abraham handed over control of the company to Samuel, who was a good businessman and saw new and different opportunities for the growing company. One of his first acts was to bid on the government mail contract for Bermuda, and he got it!

Bold and imaginative thinkers could see that the shipping industry was on the verge of a new era. The steam engine had been invented, and had already been adapted for land travel by railroad. It was obvious even then that the steam engine would also — eventually — power ships. But the big shipping companies preferred to stick to their fast, efficient, and beautiful clipper ships. Perhaps they held off for too long, which provided an opening to an adventurous entrepreneur like Samuel Cunard. He had already been one of the major investors in the steamship *Royal William*, built to link Halifax and Quebec. However, the *Royal William* was sold to a buyer in England and was sent across the ocean "under its own steam." It carried a number of passengers on its transatlantic voyage. It was this combination of "transatlantic passenger-travel and steam" that fired the imagination of Samuel Cunard.

Cunard very daringly entered a bid with the British government to carry the mail between Britain and North America — even before he had the ships to do it. His plan was to build three ships that would provide the British government with twice monthly mail service between Britain and North America, with Boston as the main North American port and branch lines to Quebec and Halifax. Cunard's three steamships would carry not only the mail across the Atlantic, but also passengers. Knowing what he wanted — speed and reliability — he contracted Robert Napier, a brilliant Scottish shipbuilding engineer, to build the ships, which were to be side paddle wheelers like the Mississippi riverboats.

With his bold and risky bid and tight time schedules, this upstart colonial from Halifax got the royal mail contract for England, and thus launched not only his new ships and a new career, but also the great century of transatlantic steamship travel.

The first of these three new ships was the *Britannia*, which was 90 metres long, had two steam-driven side paddle wheels and accommodation for 115 passengers and one cow (for fresh milk). The *Britannia* left Liverpool, England, on July 4, 1840, and arrived in Halifax 12 days later . . . two days ahead of schedule!

While it was neither the fastest nor the most luxurious ship (in fact, it was somewhat Spartan in its accommodation for passengers), it was the first steamship to carry passengers across the Atlantic on a regular run.

When the *Britannia* arrived in Boston, there was a huge public reception that they called "Cunard Festival Day." The event was as important to the city of Boston as it was to Samuel Cunard. The North American terminus was eventually moved to New York, a much larger city with an all-weather port, both of which are important factors for reliability and access to a larger passenger market. By 1848, Cunard steamships were crossing the Atlantic on a weekly service, in both directions, all year round.

Cunard's major business interests were now centred in England, so he consolidated the management of his shipping operations there, and moved to England with his family.

Even though ships like the *Great Eastern* had proven that steel hulls would eventually replace wooden hulls, Cunard's customary caution about passenger safety kept him in wooden hulls and side paddle wheelers until the problems of iron hulls and screw propellers had been worked out by his competitors. The first Cunard iron hull screw propeller ships were the *Andes* and *Alps*, built mainly for the huge immigrant trade.

When war broke out in the Crimea in 1854, Cunard's contract with Britain required him to loan some of his ships to the British Admiralty. This should have given a huge advantage to Cunard's competitors, such as the Collins Line from the United States, since they were not involved in the war. But the Collins Line had experienced two major sea disasters with a huge loss of life, and they were forced out of business.

At the end of the Crimean War, Cunard still ruled the Atlantic, and his ships still held the "Blue Ribbon," which was the unofficial measure of the supremacy of the sea for the passenger line with the best crossing time. Other lines held the Blue Ribbon from time to time, but it always came back to the Cunard Line because the Cunard Line continued to improve in every way.

For his contribution to the Crimean War effort, Cunard was made a baronet — which was a long way for the son of a penniless immigrant to Halifax to have travelled in life.

From the cramped, candle-lit passenger accommodation of Cunard's first ocean-going passenger ship, the *Britannia*, to the last great Cunard ocean liner, the *Queen Elizabeth II*, there was a vast gulf, not just in time but in size, opulence, speed, safety, and comfort. The last of the great ships were floating palaces that conjured up images from Coleridge's poem "In Xanadu did Kubla Khan a giant pleasure dome decree . . ."

No, the *Titanic* was not a Cunard ship. It belonged to the rival White Star Line, and at the time, it was the grandest ship ever built. But when the *Titanic* sank on its maiden voyage, it was a major setback to the White Star Line, and once again, the Cunard Line was supreme on the Atlantic.

It was Samuel Cunard's caution that made his line the safest on the seas. That caution served both the passengers and the ship owners; travellers were attracted by the assurance that safe travel was possible and practical. Travel by ocean liners remained the safest, most practical mode of transportation until the 1950s and 1960s when the advent of the super jet airliners closed the crossing time from days to hours, and slowly eclipsed the great ships as transatlantic people-carriers of choice.

But it was a great era that made mass travel possible. And Samuel Cunard and his ships proved that the "Blue Ribbon" meant more than speed.

George Edouard Desbarats and William Leggo

Pioneers and Inventors: Halftone Printing Process and Photojournalism

Their partnership led to a number of successful collaborations, the first of which was "Leggotype."

It has been said that destiny drives all men. But it helps if you start at the top. That was certainly true of George Edouard Desbarats.

He was born in 1838, into a family from the wealthy and privileged class of Quebec City, which gave him a head start up the rungs of the ladder of success. His father, a successful printer and publisher in pre-Confederation Canada, was also the Queen's Printer, a post that he held until his death in 1864. It was not only an honoured title, but also a guarantee of continuing government contracts to produce public documents, and it provided a source of considerable income.

After a traditional classical education, George Edouard studied law and was called to the Lower Canada Bar in 1859. He was only twenty-one years old — a very young age to become a lawyer in Quebec, even then. But George had other plans, too. The first was a "grand tour" of Europe, which he took in the following year.

When he returned, instead of pursuing law, he chose to enter the printing–publishing business of his father. By the time his father died in 1864, George Edouard had acquired a solid working knowledge of all facets of the business. Earlier in 1864, the government of the United Provinces of Canada moved to Ottawa, and as Queen's Printer, the firm followed the government there.

The Desbarats firm set up their company on the ground floor of a building on Sparks Street owned by George Edouard's father. The upper floors were rented out as an apartment building.

One of the tenants was Thomas D'Arcy McGee, one of the Fathers of Confederation. McGee had been born in Ireland, and both as a journalist and politician, he was an outspoken critic of the Fenians, a secret American-Irish society devoted to the independence of Ireland — by any means. After denouncing their activities in parliament in 1868, McGee was attacked and assassinated in the doorway of his apartment building in front of the Desbarats' printing shop on April 2. This notorious act was one of the few political assassinations in Canada, and it shocked the young nation. It also had a devastating effect on McGee's friend and landlord George Edouard Desbarats, who was moved to put up a plaque to his memory on the building.

Seven months later, the building itself was set on fire and razed to the ground with all the presses and the printing work in progress. Whether this was the reason George Edouard eventually chose to leave Ottawa is not known, but he did have extensive publishing and printing interests in both Montreal and Quebec City, which he continued to operate while he lived in Ottawa.

Now this story is not just about Desbarats, it is also about his Quebec partner William Leggo, an engraver and an inventor of some significance, but one who has not yet received the public acknowledgement he deserves!

William Leggo was the son of a German immigrant who had been trained as a printer and engraver by the master lithographers of Munich. William Leggo was trained initially by his father in the family business in Quebec. He then continued his training in Boston and Montreal. He returned to Quebec to set up his own engraving business, and it was then that he first met George Desbarats.

The two men eventually went into partnership, setting up a printing–publishing operation in Montreal. That partnership eventually led to a number of successful collaborations, the first of which was a joint patent application for what was called "Leggo-type." This was a photo-engraving process to reproduce photographed line drawings from a printing press. Leggo was the inventor; Desbarats was the promoter and financier, and significantly, also had the vision to modernize journalism with the new techniques made available through the magic of photography. Desbarats knew what he wanted, and Leggo found the way to make it work. It cost almost $250,000 (which would be worth even more now!) to develop Leggotype and it nearly bankrupted Desbarats, but he was undaunted in his pursuit of modernizing the printing industry. On several occasions over his years in publishing, Desbarats was to find himself on the brink of economic disaster.

In June of 1869, Leggo took his process a step further by taking out a patent for granulated photography, a process which created the means to convert a photo to a format that could be reproduced mechanically on a printing press. Four months later, on October 30, 1869, Desbarats introduced a new weekly news magazine called the *Canadian Illustrated News* patterned along the lines of the *London Illustrated News*, but with a difference. Instead of using line drawings to illustrate his stories, he used photographs, including a full-cover photo reproduction of Prince Arthur, the son of Queen Victoria. It was the first time a photo had ever been used anywhere in the world in any journal or newspaper of any kind.

How do you print a photograph made up of gradations of light, shade, and shadow on a printing press that prints only solid colours? This was the dilemma for publishers in the mid-nineteenth century, when photography first appeared on the scene. Photographs presented incredible new opportunities to add realism and immediacy to publications — but only if the technical problems of reproduction could be worked out.

If you take a magnifying glass and look closely at a printed photograph in any newspaper, you will see that the ink does not fully cover the image, but that the photograph is made up of dots of varying size. These dots record the intensity of the shadings of black and white in the picture. Small dots broadly spaced for the near-whites and larger dots more tightly spaced for the near-blacks. The dots are so small that your eye does not register the *individual dots,* but rather the *composite of dots* that produces the miraculous illusion of a reproduced photographic image. This is now known as the dot matrix or halftone method of printing. The process has been refined and sophisticated, but it is still the process in use today. It seems so simple when you know how it is done, but it was an incredibly ingenious method of solving a mechanical printing problem.

Other journals or newspapers are often acknowledged as being the first "daily," or "monthly," or "annual" to use photojournalism. However, the frequency and timing of these publications are irrelevant. It is the introduction of the technique and its first application to photojournalism that is important, and that distinction belongs to Desbarats and Leggo and their *Canadian Illustrated News*.

Although patents for similar techniques were issued in several other countries in the late 1870s, it is clear from the Canadian Archives and the historical record that Leggo and Desbarats were already using their photo-reproduction technique almost a decade before it was reinvented elsewhere.

During that time, Leggo's and Desbarats' *Canadian Illustrated News* and its companion French language journal *L'Opinion Publique*, covered the national news: political issues; the building of the railway; the development of cities, transportation, and industry; the opening of the west; sports events; children's issues; and fashion. In fact, they reported on almost all the things you would expect to find in a modern news magazine like *Maclean's* or *Time.* But they were "the first to see the world through the lens of a camera."

On the downside, the process was extremely expensive, and it was difficult to turn a profit with the limited subscription possibilities in the Montreal market. With this in mind, Desbarats and Leggo turned their sights on the huge market in New York, which was the centre of the world at the time. In 1873, with the backing of several prominent Canadians, they launched the *New York Daily Graphic*, which was the world's first photo-illustrated daily. So, while the United States can quite rightly claim the first "daily" newspaper to use photo illustrations, it was the same Canadian duo of Leggo and Desbarats who did it.

Desbarats had a real promotional flair. When he and Leggo launched their newspaper in New York, they created quite a "splash" . . . literally. One of the special events they sponsored was a "spectacular but unsuccessful attempt to cross the Atlantic in a balloon." However, Desbarats' enthusiasm for balloons was not unique. Their special appeal persists, and even in the current age of jet planes, there are still people trying to cross the Atlantic in balloons today.

While the techniques of publishing and printing were very important to him, so too was the substance of his publishing. He considered himself to be a publisher of quality work. He took great pride in what he produced, including a six volume history of Samuel Champlain (the great French explorer) and a *History of the Railway from Montreal*. He started the *Canadian Medical and Surgical Journal;* the *Canadian Patent Office Records and Mechanics Magazine; Hearthstone* (a Canadian literary weekly); the *Dominion Illustrated* (in which he used halftone picture engravings for the first time in Canada); and the *Dominion Printer*. He thought of himself as a pioneer of new printing techniques that would make published materials more immediate, real, and relevant to the reading public. Desbarats usually had so many activities going on at one time that it was hard to imagine how he could do them all.

His New York adventure with the *Daily Graphic* was financially disastrous almost from the beginning, because it can be costly to be a pioneer — in any field. The paper was eventually taken over by some of his financial backers, and he returned to Montreal, financially ruined. It also marked the end of his exceptional collaboration and partnership with Leggo, who stayed on in New York.

During his lifetime, Desbarats held the post of Queen's Printer in pre-Confederation Canada and was asked by his friend John A. Macdonald to serve as the Queen's Printer for the "new" Canada after Confederation. He did so, but only briefly.

When he moved to Ottawa, he built an elegant, greystone mansion on the corner of Chapel Street and Daley Avenue, which he called "Winterholme." The building still stands today on its original site near the University of Ottawa. It has been converted into an apartment building, but in its day, it was the scene of many elegant balls and soirées that attracted both the politicians and the elite of Ottawa. When Desbarats finally left Ottawa to go to Montreal in 1870, he sold his beautiful home to his friend Sir Sandford Fleming, who is the subject of another essay in this book.

So the next time you read a weekly news journal, and actually see the dots in the photos, think of Desbarats and Leggo, the team who first opened up the vast visual vista of modern photojournalism by making this now-commonplace process possible.

Charles Fenerty

Inventor: Newsprint from Wood Fibres

It was clear by the middle of the nineteenth century that a new source of basic vegetable fibre suitable to feed the demand for good quality paper had to be found.

From the earliest evidence of humans on this Earth there seems to have been a compelling need by them to record their presence here. From the primitive but powerful 10,000-year-old pictograms of humans and animals on the walls of underground caves in Lescaux, France, to the inscriptions carved in stone by ancient peoples world-wide, the method and media for recording remained essentially the same. But walls and stones and clay are cumbersome means for written communication. With the development of written languages, there was a growing need for something to record on that was simpler and more portable.

The written word changed the centuries-old oral tradition of passing down the history of the world's people. But written languages created a need for simpler and more portable writing materials.

The first form of paper appears to have been developed by the Egyptians in the sixth century B.C., using the papyrus reeds that grew along the banks of the Nile River. They used a process that is very similar to paper making today. Papyrus was not only the earliest form of paper known, but it also gave paper its name. The Chinese, on the other side of the world, independently developed hand-made paper in the second century B.C. and it was made in essentially the same way as paper is today. In both the East and the West, "paper" was scarce, expensive, and for the use of society's elite.

The ancient Greeks and Romans developed a great body of written works, including literature, history, philosophy, and mythology. Their documents were written by hand on parchment (dried animal skin) and papyrus scrolls, the paper equivalents of the time.

As literacy spread, the demand for the printed word increased, and hence, the demand for "paper." In 1798, French inventor Nicholas Louis Robert invented a mechanical paper manufacturing process. But the continuing demand for the printed word soon strained the supply of quality rags used to make the paper. It was clear by the middle of the nineteenth century that a new source of basic vegetable fibre suitable to feed the demand for good quality paper to supply the voracious mechanical presses had to be found.

Where does Charles Fenerty fit into all of this?

He was born in 1821, in Upper Falmouth, Nova Scotia. While Charles was growing up, his father owned three sawmills in the district, giving the young Charles the opportunity to spend much of his spare time at the sawmills and to learn a great deal about wood and wood fibres. He also had the opportunity as a teenager to visit the nearby Holland Paper Mill, where he learned not only the processes of paper manufacturing, but also that the growing demand for paper had almost exhausted the available supply of rags, from which paper was still made at the time.

Young Fenerty understood that the basic vegetable fibre in paper was provided by the cotton and linen in the rags. Since he also understood that wood was a vegetable fibre, he set about the task of making paper from wood fibre instead of rag fibre. From his knowledge of the paper-making process at the Holland Paper Mill, he knew he had to find a way to turn wood into a basic, workable fibrous material.

He had observed in the sawmills that the finest wood substance was the "fuzzy," almost lint-like residue that was produced from the wooden saw frame as it rubbed against the wooden slides, when it rose and fell for each new cut of lumber. Charles carefully collected and worked this fine wood residue by hand, and he followed all the same known processes of wetting, bleaching, moulding, flattening, and shaping that were used with a rag base at the paper mill.

From the residue and processing, he produced a small quantity of pulp wood paper in 1838, which he showed to his family, friends, and neighbours. None of them understood the true significance of his invention at the time. Since he was only in his late teens, the idea of patenting his invention — even the *need* to patent his invention — never crossed his mind. However, he continued to believe that it was an important breakthrough in the paper-making process because of increasing demands for paper and the diminishing supply of rags.

Regrettably, he did not make his invention broadly known beyond his own community until he sent a letter and a sample of his product to the *Acadian Recorder*. The letter was subsequently published on October 26, 1844. In his letter, Fenerty wrote that his enclosed sample "is as firm in its texture, as white, and to all appearances as durable as the common wrapping paper made from hemp, cotton or the ordinary materials of manufacture, is actually composed of spruce wood reduced to pulp and subjected to the same treatment as paper."[1] Unfortunately for Fenerty's future, fame, and fortune, around the same time that his letter was published, a similar process was patented by Freiderich Keller, a German paper-maker from Saxony.

No commercial notice was taken of Fenerty's invention until the American Civil War created a critical shortage of cloth. At that point, a number of manufacturers began making paper from wood pulp, including John Thompson of Napanee, Ontario, and another paper producer in Valleyfield, Quebec. Despite the fact the process was started in Nova Scotia, it was not until 1875 (almost 40 years after Fenerty's first successful experiments) that a wood pulp paper mill was established there in Fenerty's home province.

It is possible that Fenerty was just slightly ahead of his time. Perhaps it was merely the changing circumstances and the dimin-

[1] Francess G. Halpenny, General Editor. *Dictionary of Canadian Biography* Vol. XII, 1891–1900, (Toronto: University of Toronto Press, 1960), p. 312.

ishing availability of raw materials that finally made his paper from wood a workable alternative to the status quo of paper from rags, which had existed for 1700 years.

There is no record of Fenerty having invented anything else in his lifetime, although his life seems to have been eventful in other ways. He was a poet of note, a farmer, a social worker, an anti-smoking activist, a health warden, a tax collector, a lay church reader, a staunch Conservative, a temperance advocate, an Australian miner — and somewhat of an eccentric. He was noted for leaving his horse and buggy behind somewhere and walking home. "Once he was so engrossed in his thoughts that he could not recall at which of several locations he had become a pedestrian."[2]

The importance of Charles Fenerty's invention is as clear as the written word! The newspaper you read, the magazine you buy, the letters you write, and the page you are reading now are the legacy of Charles Fenerty, a simple man with a simple idea that helped to change the recording habits of the world.

[2] Halpenny, p. 312.

Reginald Aubrey Fessenden

Pioneer and Inventor: Radio and Electronic Communication Devices

Radio has come to mean a whole lot more in our modern world: talk radio, DJs, easy listening, sports and weather on the hour.

On my first trip to Bermuda several years ago, the helpful taxi driver who picked me up at the airport pointed out interesting sights along the way. On learning that I was a Canadian, he began to list all the famous Canadians who had lived in Bermuda. As we passed the small cemetery at St. Mark's Church, east of Hamilton, he told me that the famous Canadian inventor of the radio, Reginald Fessenden, was buried there. The driver knew something that most Canadians did not. And he was right. Reginald Fessenden did invent the radio; at least, the kind of A.M. radio we turn on each day to hear the news. And Fessenden *should* be famous, but he is not.

But mythology plays tricks with us all, and what history tells us happened is generally what we believe happened. That is certainly true of the radio. If you were to consult the historical record on the development of the radio, you would find that Guglielmo Marconi is credited with this invention. In September of 1900, he successfully sent the first wireless sound signal from Signal Hill in

St. John's, Newfoundland, and it was received at Land's End in England some 3,200 kilometres away. It was the first electrical transmission of "sound" over distance, without the aid of wires or cable — hence, "wireless." However, the sound that was transmitted was a "buzz" that had no recognizable pattern like a voice or a musical instrument.

If we were to listen to the news on the Marconi radio, we would probably be listening to a series of dots and dashes. While it could clearly convey coded messages quickly and thereby improve communications immensely, it did not present a very interesting prospect for a mass radio listening audience. And it certainly was not talk radio, DJs, easy listening, sports on the hour, and all that! But rather than debate who really invented the radio, it is probably more important to put the definition of radio itself into perspective. In the early years of electronics, radio meant the transmission of a sound signal over distance unaided by wires. While many other scientists were working along parallel lines at the time, including Edison, Fessenden, and Hertz, it was Marconi who received the radio patent on his device, which conformed to the definition of radio at the time. But radio has come to mean a whole lot more than that in our modern world. Today, it means the transmission, reception, and complete duplication of a recognizable sound sent by wireless, and it was Fessenden who invented that form of radio.

Fessenden was one of the most innovative, original thinkers in the rapidly evolving world of electronics. By the time he made his first radio broadcast, he already held patents on a number of important inventions. His big breakthrough came on Christmas Eve in 1906, when he made the world's first long-distance, wireless voice transmission from Boston, Massachusetts, to the United Fruit Company's fleet of ships, some 1,280 kilometres away in the Caribbean. Fessenden had provided the fleet with the receiving sets, and had told them they would receive a message. But they were all amazed to hear Fessenden's voice talking to them, and then singing Christmas carols while he accompanied himself on the violin! It was the world's first broadcast, and it not only redefined radio, but launched the new era of mass electronic communication that would lead to the development of the modern radio and television broadcasting industry.

So, people who like to tune in to their favourite Morse code radio station in the morning are of the Marconi school of radio, while those who like to hear voices, music, and the news are of the Fessenden school of radio. But why didn't Fessenden's invention make him instantly famous? Why did Marconi win the Nobel Prize in 1909 for his "buzz," when the "other" invention — the one that launched the era of modern radio — had already been introduced in 1906? These are curious questions for historians, giant corporations, and perhaps even patent offices.

Reginald Aubrey Fessenden was born in East Bolton, Quebec, in 1866. After a traditional Canadian education, he was employed briefly as the principal of Whitney Institute in Bermuda. There he met Helen Trott, the daughter of a prominent Burmudian. They were married in 1890.

However, in Bermuda, Fessenden felt somewhat restricted and isolated from the rest of the world and its latest advancements. He wanted to get into the fast-emerging world of electricity and electronic communication.

In Fessenden's view, the best way to do that was to work for the most successful inventor in the field at the time: Thomas Edison. He wrote to Edison, telling him that he was good at mathematics, and although he didn't know anything about electricity, he was anxious to learn. Apparently Edison was having a bad day when he received Fessenden's letter, because he promptly wrote back to him, saying "I already have too many people who don't know anything about electricity."[1]

He persisted in his attempt to join Edison, and Edison eventually hired him as a chemist at his Llewellyn Park Labs in New Jersey. This appeared to provide Fessenden with the facilities, the financial support, and the freedom to pursue the many clever ideas that "bubbled" around in his head, so he moved to the United States. However, Fessenden's collaboration with Edison was brief. Their association was brought to an abrupt end when temporary financial difficulties forced Edison to "downsize." Fessenden was one of those let go. Nonetheless, it had been an exciting and stimulating period in Fessenden's life, for which he would always be grateful. Years later, when Fessenden was asked to name the two greatest inventors of all time, without hesitation, he named Archimedes and Edison.

In 1890, Fessenden was appointed head of the electrical engineering department of Purdue University. He later held the same

---

[1] Arthur Kennedy, Jr. *The Bermudian,* August 1932.

position at the University of Pittsburgh. During his academic career, he continued his work on a number of important inventions and initiated his wireless experiments.

He left the academic life in 1909 to become a full-time inventor, and he devoted almost all his time to perfecting his electronic inventions. In 1900, when Marconi was sending his "buzz sound" across the ocean, Fessenden had already perfected his wireless voice telephone transmissions over short distances of up to 1.6 kilometres (one mile), and had received a patent for it. It was the precursor of the radio.

In the early years of the twentieth century, when the concept of radio was in its infancy, even the scientists involved did not fully understand the principles of sound transmission. The generally held notion by the scientists of the day — a notion espoused and promoted by Marconi — was the "whiplash theory." The "whiplash theory" proposed that "radio transmissions were brief, sudden impulses created by the violence of the electric spark which shot out like the sound of a whip cracked in the air...."[2] Fessenden, unlike most of his colleagues, thought that radio waves moved outward in ever-widening concentric circles from the transmitter source, like water ripples on a pond. These waves could then be used to transmit not just Marconi's "buzz," but also recognizable sounds, like a voice or music. Edison told him that this was about as likely "as a man flying to the moon." As it turned out, Fessenden was eventually proven right, even though he was generally alone in his belief in this principle at the time. (And in 1969, a man did fly to the moon!) In 1902, Fessenden formed his own Wireless Telegraph Company of Canada; and in 1906, putting his theories into practice, Fessenden made his landmark radio voice transmission.

That alone should have assured his place in history, but fame and recognition are capricious things. The world was slow to recognize the full import of what he had done that was different than his competitors.

Fessenden went on to invent a whole host of defining electronic devices, including the electro-gyro compass for submarines, the electro-gyroscopic gunsight for warships, the turbo electric drive for ships, the wireless compass, and the high frequency alternator.

---

[2] From the obituary of Reginald Aubrey Fessenden. *New York Herald Tribune*, July 22, 1932.

He also developed "tracer bullets," which have phosphorous in the outer skin of every sixth bullet in the round.

In 1912, the *Titanic* (the largest luxury ocean liner of its time), hit an iceberg in the North Atlantic, and 1,522 people died in the disaster. After this tragedy, Fessenden invented a sonar system that enabled ships at sea to detect underwater objects like icebergs or submerged rocks. Fessenden's sonar system became standard ship equipment from that point on. In addition to radio communication, Fessenden was also one of the first to carry out early experiments in television, and he understood that television would be the way of the future.

In all, he was credited with more than 500 inventions, which made him one of the most prolific and successful inventors of the modern era, and one of the true giants of the electronic communication world. And he was an excellent golfer.

Fessenden was a big man in stature as well, with a theatrical flair — from his white suits and black-lined Inverness capes, to his ever-present cigar, to his white beard. He was not at all the image of a shy and diffident Canadian.

Although recognition was slow in coming, Fessenden was awarded the Scientific American Gold Medal in 1929. And after years of litigation, he collected a settlement of $2.5 million from the Radio Trust of America for his contribution to the development of the Radio Corporation of America (RCA).

Fessenden retired to Flatt's Inlet, near Hamilton, Bermuda. He died there in 1932. And as my taxi driver had quite rightly pointed out, Fessenden is indeed buried in St. Mark's Church Cemetery. The inscription on the tombstone is simple: "His mind illumined the past . . . and the future and wrought greatly for the present. By his genius distant lands converse and men sail unafraid upon the deep."

In persisting in his belief that radio waves could carry "real" sound (despite most of his peers' views to the contrary), Fessenden created "our world of radio." And there are few of us who are not touched daily by his invention.

The *New York Herald Tribune* obituary of Reginald Fessenden said, "It sometimes happens, even in science that one man can be right against the world. Professor Fessenden was that man."[3]

[3] From the obituary of Reginald Aubrey Fessenden. *New York Herald Tribune*, July 22, 1932.

Sir Sandford Fleming

Pioneer and Inventor: Transcontinental Railway and Standard Time System

In addition to extending the railway across Canada, Fleming also invented the notion of 24 standard time zones.

While most Canadians know more about American history than they do about Canadian history, there are some Canadian historical icons that most Canadians do recognize immediately. One of them is the photo of "the last spike" being driven in to complete the Canadian Pacific Railway in 1885. Everyone knows the photograph: Several dark-clad men in hats watch as a similarly clad, frail-looking man, with a white beard, drives home the last spike with a sledgehammer. But few would be able to name any of the participants. A "point-of-view" historian once said the men in the last spike photograph were "a bunch of old guys in white beards." But they really were much more than that. They were some of the historical giants of their time — the people who built this country and set it on the road to greatness. The man driving home the spike was Donald Smith (later to become Lord Strathcona), president of the Canadian Pacific Railway. To his right was William Cornelius Van Horne, general manager of the railway.

And directly behind him was Sandford Fleming, the chief surveyor and engineer of the railway.

A Scottish immigrant to Canada, Fleming contributed to the development of Canada in many ways. In addition to his contribution to building the national railway, Fleming also invented the notion of standardizing time around the world into 24 time zones.

Sandford Fleming was born in Kirkcaldy, Fifeshire, Scotland. He arrived in Canada when he was only 17 years old, with some training in surveying and engineering. He completed his education in Canada and set himself up as a land surveyor. One of his first jobs was to survey the Toronto harbour. He did most of the work himself, charting the harbour bottom from a rowboat in summer, and through the ice in winter. During this period, he also laid out townsites, cemeteries, and roads, and he designed schools and churches. He was eventually called on to do a survey for a railroad, going from Toronto to Barrie on the Ontario, Simcoe and Huron Railway.

When he had first arrived in Canada, in 1845, there were only about 25 kilometres of railway track in the whole country. When he was called on to do the Ontario, Simcoe and Huron Line survey, there wasn't a whole lot more! Fleming started his railway work just at the beginning of the railway boom in Canada. And only 35 years after Fleming's first railway survey, Canada saw a transcontinental railway completed.

Fleming eventually became the chief engineer for the Northern Railway. Firmly established as the leading railway surveyor in Canada, he was also asked to prepare a survey for the Intercolonial Railway that would connect, what is today, Ontario, Quebec, New Brunswick, and Nova Scotia. He also became the chief engineer for the construction of the Intercolonial Railway, and while that was still in progress, he was asked to do the survey work for a railway in Newfoundland, which was a separate colony of Great Britain at that time.

In 1857, Fleming wrote a pamphlet titled "A Railway to the Pacific Through British Territory," outlining his own vision for the future. By then, the United States were developing their own national railways, and the Canadian government was becoming concerned about the British colonies in the west. After Confederation, in 1867, Prime Minister John A. Macdonald, who was another Scottish immigrant, decided it was time to act. He hired Fleming to do a broad survey and feasibility study on how Canada should build its railway.

Fleming carried out his survey over a 17-month period. Enduring all kinds of weather along the way, Fleming travelled on horseback, by canoe, and on foot over barren prairies, through rugged mountain passes in the Rockies, and through virgin wilds in northern Ontario. In all his surveying work through what was largely wilderness, Fleming worked with his men in the field, taking the same risks and surviving the same hardships they did. Fleming himself was a big, strong, rugged man, with an iron constitution, and he thrived in that sort of environment. However, 40 of his men lost their lives in completing this dangerous and formidable survey.

Fleming's preference was to take the railway line through the northern Yellowhead Pass because of its lower elevation and gentler slope. However, Donald Smith decided to take the line through Calgary; then through the Rogers, Kicking Horse, and Eagle Passes; and finally on to Vancouver and Burrard Inlet — even though there was no clear indication that this route was feasible, practical, or even usable all year round. But it was closer to the U.S. border and would not only confirm Canada's claim on the territories, but would also provide easier access to American markets. The government said the railway was about nation-building, and W.C. Van Horne said it was about making money for the private investors in the railway. They were both right, and the southern route best served both purposes.

Nonetheless, Fleming was astounded that they had ignored his recommendation for the route through the northern Yellowhead Pass. (Perhaps not surprisingly, Fleming's route was the route later taken by the Canadian National Railway.) However, Smith had sent another survey team, headed by Major A. B. Rogers, to look at the southern route. Rogers came back and said he had found the "secret" passage. One of the directors pointed out that Fleming had already mapped this route several years earlier, and it had been "documented and condemned . . . but this did not deter the indefatigable Major who proceeded to discover it again."[1]

1

David Cruise and Alison Griffiths. *Lords of the Line* (Markham: Penguin Books Canada Ltd., 1988) p. 105.

Van Horne was not impressed with Rogers' report, and he sent Fleming out once again to reconfirm the route through the Rogers Pass, which they eventually took for clearly expedient reasons. And in the end, with the driving of the "last spike," Fleming's dream of a railway across British North America became a reality.

But Fleming's significant role in building the Canadian Pacific Railway was not his only contribution to our modern world of transportation. In the course of his travels across long distances, made shorter by railways and steamships, it had become clear to Fleming's tidy mind that every town, every city, every region seemed to be operating on a different time clock. This was never a problem before because no one travelled far enough or fast enough for a synchronized time system to be important. It was important now, and Fleming decided to do something about it.

In 1878, he attended a meeting of the British Association for the Advancement of Science, in Dublin, at which he had expected to present his paper on "Standard Time." But there was not enough time on the agenda for what his British colleagues, who lived in one time zone, thought was unimportant. And he was bumped off the agenda along with his topic.

Undeterred, he spoke to his friend the Marquis of Lorne (who was not only the Governor General of Canada, but was also the son-in-law of Queen Victoria). The Marquis of Lorne had Fleming's topic bumped back on the agenda by sending copies of Fleming's paper to all the national governments of the world.

The Russian Czar Nicholas II responded and called for a world conference in Venice to discuss Fleming's idea. Fleming attended on behalf of Canada and outlined his proposal that there be a "standard" time system in which there would be 24 successive time zones around the world. It was met with general approval, and a larger meeting was called for Washington, D.C., in October 1884. The proposal was approved by 25 countries, and Standard Time came into effect on January 1, 1885, just in time for the opening of the Canadian Pacific Railway.

Not all countries adopted the new standard time system immediately. In 1885, it was still a world of competing empires, and some nations were miffed because "Greenwich time" meant the time in England was taken as the starting point. Eventually, common sense prevailed, and almost every country employed this very logical system that had been proposed by this very logical man.

Fleming was a fascinating character, with interests and talents beyond land surveys and time systems. When the Canadian government was establishing a formal postal system with postage stamps as a fee for delivery, they asked Sandford Fleming to design the stamp. His design was the famous "three-penny beaver," and it was printed in red ink on a stamp similar to those in use today. Fleming believed that the beaver symbolized industriousness and the taming of the Canadian wilderness. This was the first of many times that the beaver would be used as a symbol of Canada. It was such an effective symbol that it was later adopted by the Canadian Pacific Railway in their corporate logo. Today, the beaver is still found on the reverse side of a Canadian five-cent piece (nickel). But it was Sandford Fleming who used it first.

He was an ardent nationalist . . . and an ardent royalist. It is said that in 1849 when the parliament buildings in Montreal were burning, Fleming dashed through the flames to save the portrait of Queen Victoria. That same portrait now hangs in the parliament buildings in Ottawa. Queen Victoria expressed her gratitude by knighting him in 1897.

Fleming was a charter member of the Royal Society of Canada and was the founder of the Canadian Institute. Appropriately, for an ardent royalist, he was the Chancellor of Queen's University. In addition, he had a pocketful of honorary degrees from all over the world. It was said that Fleming, a man of broad interests and great energy, was equally at home in the wilderness or in the grand salons of Europe.

And he is one of Canada's historical icons and should be remembered by all of us. If you have ever taken a train, travelled through time zones, or posted a letter, you have followed in the footsteps of Sir Sandford Fleming.

Dr. Abraham Gesner

Pioneer and Inventor: Kerosene and Petrochemical Industry

He called his product "Kerosinite" and eventually shortened it to "kersone," which has remained the product's name to this day.

Before the era of corporate sponsors with enormous budgets for large-scale research and development, invention was largely a solitary occupation, carried out by people who often had to make personal sacrifices for their experimental work, and often had to use their own money to finance it!

Dr. Abraham Gesner, the inventor of kerosene and a pioneer in geology and the petrochemical industry, was one such inventor. Larger than life in many respects, Gesner was a big, muscular man, with boundless energy, almost unlimited talent, and a multi-faceted personality. He was also a true eccentric.

Born in Nova Scotia, educated in Canada and England, and employed in Canada and the United States, Abraham Gesner died in 1864, and was largely forgotten by the middle of the twentieth century. But not by everyone!

Gesner was well known to historians and to the petrochemical industry. And to their great credit, Imperial Oil of Canada, which owned a massive refinery across Halifax Harbour from Gesner's gravesite at Camp Hill Cemetery, had a monument erected to him over his grave in 1933 to commemorate his accomplishments and to honour his memory. The monument bears these words:

"Abraham Gesner, MD, FGS, Geologist, born at Cornwallis, N.S., May 2nd, 1797. Died at Halifax, April 29th, 1864. His treatise on The Geology and Mineralogy of Nova Scotia 1836, was one of the earliest works dealing with those subjects in this province, and about 1852 he was the American inventor of the process of kerosene oil."

Throughout his childhood, Abraham Gesner showed an exceptional interest in plants, animals, and particularly rocks. By the time he was 15 years old, he was filled with the spirit of adventure, and he shipped off to sea as an ordinary sailor on a square rigger sailing ship.

But this was not at all what his well-to-do father had in mind for his son. When Abraham returned from one of his trips, his father called a family meeting that included the other eleven Gesner children. Prompted by their father, Abraham's eleven siblings agreed that Abraham should become a doctor, an occupation they considered to be far more respectable than a sailor.

So with his adventurous start in life apparently behind him, Gesner set sail for England to become a doctor and fulfill his father's wishes. In England, he found himself freed from the restraints of home. Cleverly, he not only studied medicine, but also indulged his passion for geology by taking it in his option courses at university (which is something to keep in mind).

Thus, Abraham Gesner came home a doctor, but he also came home a geologist. Throughout his life, geology remained his passion. He dutifully set up a medical practice in Cornwallis, Nova Scotia. And as was also expected of him, he married.

In a day when doctors still made house calls, Abraham did so mounted on a big black horse that became one of his trademarks. His big black horse also gave him the opportunity to carry out his geological explorations over vast regions of New Brunswick, and where his horse wouldn't go, Abraham went on foot or by canoe. As a result of his pioneer work in the geology of the region, the province appointed him the official provincial geologist in 1838, and he held that post until it was abolished in 1842.

By then, Gesner was already experimenting with the extraction of illuminating oils from coal. He called his product "Kerosinite" (from the Greek *keros*, meaning "candle wax"). He eventually shortened the word to "kerosene," which has remained the product's name to this day. His financial backer was another inventor, the Earl of Dundonald, who was then head of the British Naval Forces in Halifax. Gesner's public experiment with his kerosene in Halifax was a "brilliant" success, both figuratively and literally. The brightness of the light generated by kerosene amazed everyone who saw it, including the famous politician Joseph Howe. Howe persuaded Gesner to use it in a beach lighthouse in Halifax. The light, it was said, was so brilliant and intense, compared to other light sources in use at the time, that ships at sea actually came in to shore for a closer look.

Nevertheless, kerosene still presented Gesner with some challenges. The cost of extracting kerosene from coal was high, and there were problems with the smell and smoke that resulted from burning kerosene.

However, with his extensive knowledge of the geology of New Brunswick, he recalled a substance that was like coal (but was not coal) and that was easily extracted from the ground. In addition, it burned with a clear white intense light. The substance was called "Albertite," after Prince Albert of England.

When Gesner tried to use the substance, he ran into one of the first instances of a dispute over corporate proprietary rights. Albertite had been largely ignored by the coal conglomerate in New Brunswick because it wasn't really coal. However, when Gesner wanted to use it, he was blocked by the conglomerate because they had the coal extraction rights for the province. A court case ensued, and the conglomerate brought in their "outside experts," who claimed that Albertite was now coal. Gesner lost the case, and the corporate predators and their political friends made a fortune from Gesner's discovery.

Undeterred, the ever-inventive Gesner went to Newton Creek on Long Island, New York, where he took out U.S. patents on his invention and established the North American Kerosene Gas and Light Company. Gesner's business partner eventually bought him out, making Gesner quite wealthy very late in his life. All his hard work and creativity were finally rewarded!

Gesner returned to Nova Scotia and spent the rest of his life with his rocks, his books, and his inventions. While Gesner is mainly known today for his invention of kerosene, he was a man of diverse talents and interests, comprising both arts and science. He played the flute, started Canada's first museum, and was a medical doctor, a geologist, an author, and a sailor.

While he may have played the flute, he "marched to a different drummer." His unique pioneering spirit and his dedication to geology combined with his imagination, stubbornness, and eccentricity helped him to persevere against adversity. It is somewhat ironic that even without research and development funds from a corporate sponsor, Abraham Gesner became one of Canada's major contributors to the flowering of corporate America.

Dr. Gerhard Herzberg

Research Scientist: Molecular Research (especially of Free Radicals)

His Nobel Prize did not change his fundamental pattern of life, which was still dominated by his curiosity and devotion to research.

While most scientists who search the skies at night with telescopes are looking for planets, stars, and other large bodies in the universe, others such as Gerhard Herzberg focus their search on much smaller things: atoms and molecules, the building blocks of the universe. They conduct their search with the special tools and techniques of the science of spectroscopy.

Gerhard Herzberg was born in Hamburg, Germany, in 1904. As he was growing up, he dreamed of becoming an astronomer. He was obsessed with the universe, and even built his own telescope to bring the stars closer. But his dream was not to be! His father died when Gerhard was only ten years old, and his mother could not afford to send him to the Hamburg Observatory. Instead, through an industrial scholarship, he was able to go to the Darmstadt Technical University, where he studied engineering physics and earned his Ph.D. By the time he was 24 years old, he had published 20 technical papers and, thus, had little trouble obtaining a teaching fellowship at the University of Göttingen for one year, followed by a one-year fellowship at the University of Bristol. He returned briefly to Göttingen to marry Luise Hedwig Oettinger, who had been one of his students at the university.

He then took up a lectureship at Darmstadt. He began to concentrate his studies on spectroscopy while working with other graduate students, including John Spinks of Saskatoon. Although Gerhard had never heard of Saskatoon before, it would soon become very important to him.

In 1934, Herzberg was advised that he was to be dismissed because his wife was Jewish. They knew then that they had to leave Nazi Germany. But where to go? With the flood of intellectuals fleeing Europe and an economic depression devastating North America, the prospects for teaching posts were bleak. Gerhard asked Spinks to see if there was a place for him in Canada. Neither the University of Toronto nor the National Research Council had openings, but the University of Saskatchewan, which had little money, offered him a teaching research position on Carnegie grants.

Herzberg and his wife arrived in Saskatoon with $2.50 between them. It was the beginning of one of the most satisfying periods of Herzberg's life. He wrote three of his major books in Saskatoon, and his two children were born there. It is an interesting comment about Canada and the international political climate at the time, that even though Herzberg was a refugee from Hitler, and already a renowned physicist, he was not allowed to work in the Canadian war effort because he was considered an "enemy alien." Herzberg became a Canadian citizen in 1945, at which time, he was offered a job at the Yerkes Observatory at the University of Chicago. He accepted the position, which allowed him the luxury of a well equipped facility with solid financing. He established a lab there to continue his "spectra" studies, and he began to build his own credentials as a world leader in this field.

In 1948, the National Research Council lured him away from Chicago with an opportunity to establish a lab for fundamental research in spectroscopy. It did not take much persuading because Herzberg liked Canada and the Canadian scientific community. Under his leadership, the National Research Laboratory became one of the leading facilities in the world, and it attracted a first-class team of scientists.

"Spectroscopy is the study of the unique frequencies of light that atoms and molecules emit or absorb. Because of their uniqueness (displayed on a spectral light band) these frequencies serve as 'fingerprints' that scientists can use to identify the type of atom or molecule they are observing."[1]

This field of study allowed scientists to identify molecules in outer space, pollutants in the environment and even the transient processes that occur in complex biological and chemical changes.

In 1971, Gerhard Herzberg was awarded the Nobel Prize for Chemistry for his work in spectroscopy, becoming Canada's fourth Nobel Prize recipient since the awards were first established in 1901.

Many Nobel Prize winners receive their awards for research they have carried out years — and sometimes decades — before. Herzberg's prize was awarded for the work he did during the 1950s and 1960s at the National Research Council. In the introduction to the award presentation, Dr. Claesson of the Royal Swedish Academy of Sciences explained that Herzberg had received the award "for his contribution to the knowledge of electronic structure and geometry of molecules particularly free radicals" and for his contribution to "the rapid development of molecular spectroscopy." "Herzberg's pioneering investigation of free radicals" and "knowledge of their properties is of fundamental importance to our understanding of how chemical reactions proceed."[2]

"Free radicals are fragments that are created when a chemical reaction causes a molecule to break up: they exist only for the length of time it takes them to re-arrange themselves into new molecules . . . But free radicals are difficult to study because their lifetime is so short — mere millionths of a second. Herzberg applied pioneering pulsed, spectroscopic techniques to precisely determine the structures and properties of over 30 free radicals."[3]

Even though a Nobel Prize is the ultimate recognition for a scientist, Gerhard Herzberg did not let it change his fundamental pattern of life, which was still dominated by his curiosity and his devotion to research. Under his leadership the National Research Council of Canada became, and still is today, a world leader in spectroscopy. When Herzberg stepped down from his position of

[1] Dr. Boris Stoichoff. *Physics in Canada*, Vol. 28 (April 1972) p. 3.
[2] Tylor Wasson. *Nobel Prize Winners*, (New York: W. H. Wilson Co. 1987) p. 445.
[3] Stoichoff. *Physics in Canada*, p. 3.

Director of the Division of Physics, he did not really retire. He became the first Distinguished Research Scholar of the Council, and continued to come to the office every day.

In 1970, a special Herzberg medal was designed to be given to one Canadian physicist each year for the highest achievement in physics. When he was shown the medal, he saw that on one side it had a chemical symbol, and on the other, a stamped portrait of himself. "But it doesn't look like me!" At this point, Mrs. Herzberg smiled, remembering Picasso's reply to Gertrude Stein who had said the same thing on seeing Picasso's portrait of her. With a twinkle in her eye, Mrs. Herzberg calmly remarked, "Just wait."[4]

[4] Stoichoff. *Physics in Canada*, p. 22.

Dr. Helen Sawyer Hogg

Astronomer: Variable Star Specialist and Discoverer

She popularized astronomy for countless school children . . . explaining astronomy and the stars in simplified terms.

Helen Hogg was once interviewed on a television program in Washington, D.C., and was asked by the T.V. personality what it was she did . . . exactly. When she told him that she studied the stars and the universe with her telescope, he asked her if she had brought her telescope with her. She confessed that she had not. It weighed 40 tons and had a protective revolving canopy that weighed another 80 tons!

"Her telescope," like her world, was much larger than the interviewer could imagine and far beyond anything that most people could even dream. "Her telescope" was the David Dunlap Observatory located in Richmond Hill, Ontario. When the Dunlap Observatory was opened in 1935, its 188-centimetre polished glass reflector mirror was the second largest in the world. Long before the age of human astronauts and spacecraft with telescopic cameras, it was one of the world's most powerful means of exploring the vast expanse of outer space. Hogg did just that with "her telescope" for most of her long and productive life.

Born in Lowell, Massachusetts, in 1905, Helen Sawyer saw Halley's Comet on its flight past Earth when she was only five years old. It changed her life forever! From that moment on, her life moved towards a career in astronomy, even though she would later confess that she did not really seek a career, but that circumstance and opportunity thrust one upon her. She received her Ph.D. from Radcliffe College at Harvard University. She married fellow astronomer Frank Hogg, and they both accepted positions at the Dominion Astrophysical Observatory at Victoria, B.C., in 1931. When the Dunlap Observatory was opened by the University of Toronto in 1935, Frank Hogg accepted a position there, while Helen pursued her astronomy research and lectured at the University of Toronto. When her husband died suddenly in 1951, she took over his weekly column on astronomy at the *Toronto Daily Star* and continued to write the column for more than 30 years. Through it, she popularized astronomy for countless school children (and their parents), explaining astronomy and the stars in simplified terms — to the extent that they could ever be "simplified." Some of her best columns were put together in a book titled *The Stars Belong to Everyone*. And she truly believed they did!

With *Sputnik* and the advent of human space travel, a new era of astronomy was dawning and new student interest was being kindled. Throughout her life, she dedicated herself to teaching astronomy to these new generations of eager students. But she did not neglect her own research and spent most nights scanning the heavens, developing her knowledge base in her own special field of variable stars and globular clusters. At the time of her death, over 400 variable stars had been identified, and Helen Hogg was credited with locating almost one fourth of them.

She was greatly respected and honoured during her own lifetime. She was a fellow of the Royal Society of Canada, President of the Royal Astronomical Society of Canada, President of the Royal Canadian Institute, President of the American Association of Variable Star Observers, and Program Director for Astronomy at the National Science Foundation in Washington, D.C.

In special recognition of her work, the National Museum of Science and Technology in Ottawa named its observatory after her. And in her honour, an asteroid, or minor planet, between Jupiter and Mars was named "Sawyer Hogg" by the International Astronomical Union.

She never lost the thrill of exploring the sky, and she would be the first to admit that we really know very little about the vast, mysterious space that surrounds us. Although she believed it is possible that a spaceship from beyond our world may one day appear, she also believed no scientific evidence supports the theory that one has already done so. She did not believe in astrology, and more than once crossed swords with some of its most enthusiastic adherents for not sharing their views on the universe. However, she did acknowledge that the universe affects our world in many mysterious ways beyond our own understanding.

Halley's Comet, which started her on her own space odyssey, visits Earth on its eccentric elliptical orbit about once every 76 years. Helen Hogg lived long enough to see it return in 1986.

Her life was devoted to the study of the stars. During her journey, she taught for 40 years, wrote a column for 30 years, and worked at her beloved David Dunlap Observatory until the day she died in 1993.

When she died, alas, she could not take her telescope with her. But she left behind a legacy of knowledge and experience for the new generations of astronomers who will use "her telescope" to continue and extend her work.

Dr. Harold Johns

Research Scientist and Inventor: Cobalt Bomb for Cancer Treatment

The Cobalt Bomb could bombard a tumour with the concentrated stream of radiation produced by the decay process of cobalt 60.

Harold Johns had an unconventional start in life, and he remained relatively unconventional for most of his working years. He was born in 1915, in a Buddhist Temple at a mountain-top retreat near Chandu, China, where his missionary father was a math professor at West China University. As a child, he "remembers waking up to the sound of gongs rung in front of idols."[1] He even learned to speak Mandarin Chinese before the family returned to Canada permanently when he was 12 years old. He earned a Bachelors Degree in Physics from McMaster University in 1936, and his Ph.D. from the University of Toronto in 1939. He won a scholarship to go to Cambridge, but World War II intervened, and he spent the war years at the University of

1

    Lillian Newberry. "No Rocking Chair for this Retiring Physicist" *The Toronto Star*, July 5, 1980.

Calgary, lecturing in physics and teaching military personnel the mysteries of radar.

In 1945, at war's end, Johns joined the University of Saskatchewan, where he enjoyed immense intellectual freedom and spent 11 of his most productive working years. In 1946, he was in Toronto and heard a lecture given by Dr. William Mayneord, a British physicist, who had spent the war working at Canada's nuclear research centre at Chalk River, Ontario, where he studied the biological effects of radiation. In his lecture, Mayneord indicated that radioactive cobalt was capable of producing a sufficient concentration of high energy rays to destroy cancer cells. Johns, whose interest in "biophysics" was already firmly rooted, was intrigued! But to do further studies, he would need to get the radioactive cobalt... And that required access to a nuclear reactor!

When Johns returned to Saskatchewan, he had a chat about his idea — and his dilemma — with Tommy Douglass, who was the premier of the province at the time.

Eventually, Johns was allowed to arrange for a small quantity of cobalt to be placed in the prototype nuclear reactor at Chalk River, Ontario. This provided not only the radioactive material, but also the opportunity to link his training as a physicist with his interest in radiation medicine.

Radiation therapy had been used for cancer treatment since the discovery of radium in 1898. However, the radiation voltage available from radium was proven to be so low and unfocused that it could not penetrate deeply enough beneath the skin (where most tumours were located) to have much effect. As well, the patient was expected to remain immobile for up to an hour — an almost impossible feat. And despite the low voltage, the radiation burned tissue and damaged healthy cells surrounding the tumours.

Johns was working with "Cobalt 60," which was capable of generating up to 20 times the concentrated radiation of radium. He set about developing a mechanism that could harness this new source of power. The result was his "Cobalt Bomb." It was given this name by its creators — not because it could blow up (it could not), but because its power could be focused at a single point and bombard a tumour with the concentrated stream of radiation produced by the decay process of cobalt 60.

The amount of cobalt 60 in the machine was not massive. About the size of a flashlight battery and protected by a lead jacket, the cobalt 60 was housed in an overhead unit above the patient on the table. It was mounted on a wheel that could turn to focus the radiation beam through a hole in the lead shield and onto the target area. The cobalt 60 therapy unit was installed at the University Hospital in Saskatoon, and was one of only two cobalt 60 units in the world. The other was in London, Ontario, and was supported by the recently created Atomic Energy of Canada Limited.

Johns' cobalt 60 therapy unit had a "collimating system," which gave it the ability to aim and concentrate a thin stream of radiation unwaveringly at the tumour. It was this system, in addition to the unit's careful construction, that made it so different. This prototype was the basis for the commercial units that were later produced for use all over the world. For the patient, this powerful tool reduced the treatment sessions from one hour to just five minutes. Even more important, it made deep-seated tumours more accessible to treatment.

Johns' Cobalt Bomb was put into use in 1951. Around the same time, he developed his precise depth–dose ratio tables to determine the dosage for each patient. These tables remained in use for many years until they were replaced by computer-generated tables from the Princess Margaret Hospital in Toronto.

In 1951, Johns was elected a fellow of the Royal Society of Canada. A year later, he was selected as Saskatoon's Citizen of the Year by a grateful city. In 1953, he published a book on radiation therapy titled *The Physics of Radiology*, which became the definitive work for succeeding generations. It went through a number of editions and reprints, including translations into Russian and Chinese. In 1956, Johns moved to Toronto, where he became head of the physics division of the Canadian Cancer Institute, and professor of the physics department in medical biophysics at the University of Toronto. By this time, he was known throughout the world for his exceptional contribution to medical science, and in particular, the field of cancer research and treatment.

He was also an excellent teacher. An unattributed reference in the University of Toronto archives says "[Johns'] clarity of mind and desire to communicate the excitement of science pervades his lectures so that many of Canada's leading scientists in radiation physics and radiation biology, are his former students."

In his career, he received many other honours and awards, including honorary doctorates from both McMaster University and the University of Saskatchewan. But the honour he treasured most was his Order of Canada.

His enthusiasm, drive, and energy were not restricted to his scientific work alone. He loved most sports, including golf and water-skiing. Some of his colleagues described him as a "fanatic" about squash. He was a difficult opponent to defeat at anything, and he never went down without a fight. He tried to instill these same principles in his students.

And what did Johns see in the future for cancer research and treatment? He did not see a "magic bullet" or a super drug that would make cancer go away. However, during his time, he was greatly encouraged by the important progress that was made on many fronts in the fight against cancer. He was also proud that he and his colleagues had helped to push back the clouds from the frontier, giving new life and hope to those who were helped by his "peaceful bomb."

John and Allen McIntosh

Discovery: McIntosh Apple

The apple was one in a million and a true Canadian legend in its own right!

Did you know that the McIntosh Apple really was an apple before it was a computer?

The true origin of the McIntosh apple is shrouded in mystery and our own kind of Canadian legend. However, it seems to be clear that the apple came from the McIntosh Farm at McIntosh Corners near the present-day site of Upper Canada Village along the St. Lawrence River in eastern Ontario. So at least we seem to agree on the location, and in 1912, a monument was erected on the site to firmly fix it in our minds.

Legend has it that John McIntosh, the son of a United Empire Loyalist, was the "originator" of the apple in about 1815, but there is little real evidence to support the story. The legend also says that it all started when John and his son Allen found some seedling apple trees in a clearing in the forest on their property. They transplanted the seedlings in their own small orchard, where the trees flourished. Allen is credited with recognizing the exceptional qualities of the apples on one of the trees, which he used as the breeding stock for his growing orchards. The apple was probably derived from a snow apple that by chance had produced a very special strain of the variety. "It was one in a million."[1]

The McIntosh apple fell in and out of favour with apple breeders and apple eaters during the nineteenth century. But its popularity came into its own in the twentieth century when "William Macoun, the Dominion horticulturist at the experimental farm in Ottawa affirmed the apple's outstanding suitability for the Canadian climate and the increasingly important urban market . . . it is one of the finest appearing and dessert apples grown."[2]

The McIntosh — an apple that is one in a million and a true Canadian legend in its own right!

[1] Francess G. Halpenny, General Editor. *Dictionary of Canadian Biography*, Vol. VII, (Toronto: University of Toronto Press, 1960), p. 563.

[2] Halpenny, p. 563.

John Cunningham McLennan

Research Scientist and Inventor: Commercial Production of Helium

He succeeded in liquefying helium with his modest resources in 1923, while the United States government, which had spent millions to do the same, had failed!

By the time the Wright brothers flew the first successful fixed-wing aircraft at Kitty Hawk, New Jersey in 1903, air pioneers had already been flying in balloons for over 120 years! They were mainly French.

The first recorded flight was made by Jean-François de Rozier, who flew over Paris in a hot air balloon in 1783. In 1785, Jean-Pierre Blanchard flew a hot air balloon across the English Channel. And in 1852, Henri Gifford flew over Paris in the first cigar-shaped airship powered by a steam-driven propeller — at about only 10 kilometres an hour. The first navigable airship was also of French design and was appropriately named *La France*. It was flown by Charles Renard in 1884 and used an electrically rotated propeller. But it was Count Ferdinand Von Zeppelin, a German, who designed the definitive airship in 1900, and with it, he ushered in the era of the dirigible. And they were different!

The Zeppelin airship was a sleek, cigar-shaped dirigible, with a series of independent gas bags enclosed in a light, rigid metal frame. It used the lighter-than-air but highly flammable hydrogen gas to provide the lifting capacity. It was propeller-driven by two gas engines, and had steering rudders at both the front and the rear. Two gondolas were slung beneath to carry the crew, the passengers, and the engines.

The first commercial passengers were flown by the Zeppelin airship *Deutschland* in 1910. At the time, there were many who believed that this type of aircraft held much greater commercial promise than the "heavier-than-air" fixed-wing aircraft of the Wright brothers.

By the beginning of World War I in 1914, ten such Zeppelins were in commercial passenger service in Europe, and more were in production for use by the German military. By 1915, Zeppelins were already a force to be reckoned with in the war. They made bombing raids on London and other strategic locations in eastern England. They provided unique observation posts from which the Germans could monitor British shipping and troop movements. And generally, the Zeppelins created a nuisance factor because they could go anywhere above the battle, just as submarines had been able to do under the sea. Both were a serious problem for the allies.

To deal with the changing weapons of war, the British Admiralty Board of Invention and Research sought out the leading scientists and inventors from its allies to help in its work. Among them was physics Professor John Cunningham McLennan of the University of Toronto, who was asked to investigate the rare gas helium as a possible non-flammable balloon gas to replace the volatile and dangerous hydrogen gas.

John McLennan was born in Ingersoll, Ontario, in 1867, the year of Canada's Confederation. He did his undergraduate and graduate degrees at the University of Toronto, and his post-graduate work at Cambridge University. In 1907, he was named professor of physics at the University of Toronto, where he subsequently spent the rest of his academic career. He was highly respected for his work in a number of disciplines, but he is particularly remembered for his scientific work in the war effort.

At the beginning of the war, helium was a relatively rare gas that had not been commercially produced in quantity anywhere. Therefore, it was very expensive . . . about $20,000 per cubic metre. McLennan's team found significant quantities of helium in gas wells south of Lethbridge and Medicine Hat in Alberta. McLennan, "with the assistance of staff from the University of Toronto and the University of Calgary . . . constructed and worked a semi-commercial plant in Calgary for the extraction of helium from natural gas and proved it could be produced in quantity for less than 10¢ per cubic foot. As a result, it now became practicable to use helium for the filling of airships."[1] By the end of the war, the plant was producing enough helium to provide a steady supply for the war effort, and was one of the only sources of helium in the world.

In 1917, McLennan moved to England to work full-time in the war effort, first as a technical advisor to the Admiralty Board of Invention and Research, and later in the same year, as its director. Among McLennan's accomplishments of the time was his collaborative work with renowned scientist Sir Ernest Rutherford in developing magnetic devices for detecting submarines, which were taking a terrible toll on allied ships at the time. Following the introduction of the magnetic devices, McLennan was quoted as saying that "the Admiralty can now sink subs faster than the Germans can make them."

The same might have been said of the Zeppelins, for of 67 Zeppelin airships that had been put into military service during the war, only 16 survived. The Zeppelin's fatal flaw was the hydrogen gas that was used for its lifting capacity. Hydrogen made the Zeppelin dirigible extremely vulnerable to any kind of incendiary material such as bullets, bombs, and shells.

The Zeppelin's poor survival record during the war indicated that hydrogen-filled dirigibles might be too dangerous for commercial passenger service. But in turn, that meant there might be a market for non-flammable helium, which had almost the same lifting capacity as hydrogen and would obviously be a safer choice.

As the war came to an end, Britain intensified its efforts to build a safe and practical airship. In 1919, they launched the airship R34, which was the first airship to cross the Atlantic. It used helium instead of hydrogen.

In the meantime, John McLennan had been awarded the Order of the British Empire for his scientific work in the war. In 1919, he returned to Canada to continue his work at the University of

---

[1] *The Toronto Telegram*, February 1923.

Toronto. He succeeded in liquefying helium with his modest resources in 1923, while the United States government, which had spent millions to do the same, had failed! Apart from its potential use in the airship industry and in balloons, there seemed few practical uses for helium. (The industrial value of helium in rockets, nuclear reactors, and refrigeration would not be realized for several decades.)

Nonetheless, the great age of the dirigible continued, with some manufacturers using helium, while others continued to use hydrogen. The *Graf Zeppelin* of Germany went around the world in 22 days in 1925. The British-built *R101* was an enormous airship with passenger accommodations for 100 people. Accommodations included a dining room, sleeping berths, and recreation facilities. A year later, the *R101* crashed during a storm in India and killed 46 people. At that point, Britain abandoned dirigibles for commercial passenger travel and concentrated on developing the airplane.

In 1937, after a transatlantic crossing, the Zeppelin *Hindenberg* was docking at Lakehurst, New Jersey, when a spark ignited the hydrogen gas. A flaming fire ball consumed the airship in mere minutes, killing 36 of the 90 passengers. This incident put an end to the age of the great passenger airships and marked the beginning of the domination of commercial air travel by airplanes.

While helium did not prolong the life of the lighter-than-air dirigible as a major means of passenger transportation, it did reassure a skeptical public that airships could be a viable mode of transportation. It remains one of the unexplained mysteries of the time why all airship companies did not make use of helium, once it was commercially available. Perhaps the industry was doomed in any event, not so much because of the safety of the gases used, but because of the rapid advances in technology that made the airplane a safer, faster, more reliable, and more controllable passenger-carrier.

However, one only needs to watch a weekend sports-event on television to see the modern descendant of the great airships. The Goodyear blimp that hovers over such events uses helium gas, which was made available to us through the efforts of McLennan.

In his university work, McLennan made a significant contribution to the fields of low temperature research (or cryogenics), spectroscopy, radioactivity, and the treatment of cancer by radium.

In his lifetime, McLennan received many honours, including an LL.D. from the University of Toronto. In 1915, he was made a fellow of the Royal Society of Canada, and in 1924, the president of the Royal Society.

On the personal side, McLennan was a big, friendly man, who was always impeccably dressed. He was a brilliant lecturer and speaker, with a certain theatrical flair that often left his audiences enthralled. He was extremely proud of his Canadian birth and his Scottish heritage, and he usually spent his holidays in either the Canadian Rockies or the Scottish Highlands. He retired to England in 1932. In 1935, he was knighted by the King for his "fundamental discoveries in physics, and scientific work in peace and war." He died suddenly that year, while travelling by train between Paris and Boulougne in France.

James Naismith

Inventor: Sport of Basketball

He thought an active floor game in the gymnasium would be just about right — if he could make the game interesting enough.

No, basketball was *not* invented by the Chicago Bulls and Michael Jordan! It was invented over 100 years ago by Canadian James Naismith.

Naismith was born in Almonte, Ontario, and graduated from McGill University, where he had been an outstanding athlete. After a brief period as the director of Physical Education at McGill, he moved to Springfield, Massachusetts. In 1891, Naismith was the director of Physical Education at the YMCA training school in Springfield. He had been searching for a team sport that would keep his football team in fit condition over the winter months, and he thought an active floor game in the gymnasium would be just about right — if he could make the game interesting enough.

So instead of simply setting up goal posts as in soccer, hockey, or lacrosse, Naismith decided on a smaller, unguarded target that would require some skill in scoring with a large inflated ball. He chose peach baskets as the targets, which he attached to the overhanging balcony at both ends of the gym. Hanging about three metres (10 feet) from the ground, the baskets were well out of reach of any of his players. (Obviously not high enough for today's game with its tall "airborne" players, who can easily reach the rim and "slam-dunk" the ball at that height.)

So basketball actually started with real "baskets." And even though they have evolved into cord netting that hangs from the rim of steel hoops that are firmly affixed to a backboard, they are still called "baskets," and the game is still called "basketball." But the fast and incredibly skillful game that is played today is a far cry from its humble beginnings and its Canadian roots.

Daniel David Palmer

Innovator and Pioneer: Founder of Chiropractics

He concluded logically that if "something" snapped in Lillard's back, causing immediate deafness, and, if that "something" could be put right again, his hearing should be restored.

Daniel David Palmer is credited with having developed the principles of chiropractics in 1895 in Davenport, Iowa. But he was born in Port Perry, Ontario, in 1845, and that fact is commemorated by a bronze bust and a monument in a park in central Port Perry.

Following the American Civil War in 1865, and with Canada going through difficult economic times, Daniel and his brother Thomas set out to seek their fortune in the United States, which they considered to be the land of "greater" opportunity. So, with two Canadian dollars in their pockets and great expectations in their hearts, they set out for Buffalo, New York, about 320 kilometres away . . . Walking!

They arrived in Buffalo 30 days later, and from that point on, their lives read like the stuff of great novels. They worked their way from Buffalo to "Detroit City," and from there to Chicago, where they managed to hitch a ride on a troop train headed towards Davenport, Iowa. Thomas went to Medford, Oklahoma, where he became the founder and publisher of the *Oklahoma Guardian*, the most popular newspaper in the territory. Daniel David proceeded down the Mississippi River to New Boston, Illinois, where he went into the bee-keeping and honey production business, which was highly successful according to the records of shipments to the big cities back east.

Daniel David married his housekeeper, Lavinia McGee, the widow of a Confederate Army officer who had been killed in action. They then moved to the beautifully named What Cheer, Iowa, where Daniel David (now known as "D.D.") opened a grocery store and became a fish importer. He was very successful at this enterprise. Nevertheless, he was sometimes referred to as a "fish peddler" by those who sought to discredit him later on in his life.

After eight years of marriage, and the birth of the Palmers' three children, D.D.'s wife died, leaving him alone and with no idea of what to do next.

In the nineteenth century (in both the Canadian and the American frontier territories), the practice of medicine was generally not the highly sophisticated, intellectual pursuit that it is today. (Doctors even made house calls!) Most doctors had an office, but they also tended to carry the tools of their trade with them in a small black leather bag filled with a frightening assortment of metal tools, potions, and bandages.[1]

Then as now, there existed alternative forms of medicine. Some of these alternative forms were practised by natural "magnetic healers." Magnetic healers usually eased pain and suffering with drug-free methods of healing that involved the use of their hands. A few of their remedies were not unlike some of the traditional Chinese healing methods that are still used today.

In 1885, D.D. moved to Davenport, Iowa, where he set up office as a magnetic healer which he had been practising "unofficially" for some time. His methods were based largely on positive thinking and on the human mind's effect on the body's ability to heal itself — with a little help from the outside. D.D. believed that most

[1] (In fact, my own father had one that had been handed down for generations in his family. I remember it well: an ancient, mysterious bag with ancient, mysterious tools!)

disease and illness could be healed by the natural intelligence systems inside the body, which he called the "the innate" — a healing force within us all.

D.D. Palmer was highly successful as a "magnetic healer," but in September 1885, when he was 50 years old, he made a discovery that assured him a place in history. One of his patients, Harvey Lillard, was deaf and was recounting to D.D. what had happened to him some years earlier. He had been lifting a heavy weight, and in the course of this exertion, something snapped in his back, and immediately he lost his hearing. Palmer kept copious notes on everything to do with his patients: whatever he heard, did, or saw with them. He was extremely observant (after all, his livelihood depended upon it). Upon hearing Lillard's account, he concluded logically that if "something" snapped in Lillard's back, causing immediate deafness, and if that "something" could be put right again, his hearing should be restored.

Palmer manipulated his patient's back by readjusting the vertebrae in his spine, just as chiropractors and doctors might do today. The results were immediate! With the "crack" of his back, Lillard's vertebrae snapped back into the correct position, and his hearing was restored. In D.D. Palmer's own words, what happened that day "was the birth of a new health science by the adjustment of this displaced vertebrae."[2] He called this new health science "Chiropractic," and in time, he went on to found the Palmer School of Chiropracty in Davenport, Iowa. Founding his own school did not prevent him from teaching courses at the Davenport School of Chiropracty, when it was opened some years after his own school. Palmer's son B.J. (Bartlett Joshua), who had joined his father in both his practice and teaching, thought it was heresy to help the "opposition." To D.D. Palmer, it was simply promoting chiropractics. B.J. was the hard-driving, pragmatic businessman who played golf on weekends. D.D. was "unique in his approach to life, with a disregard for conventions of society."[3] He was considered an eccentric, even by his numerous friends. Nonethless, father and son were actually much the same in their style and temperament. But D.D. Palmer's easy-going attitude

[2] David D. Palmer. *The Palmers: The Memoirs of Daniel D. Palmer* (Davenport: Bauslin Brothers, 1978), p. 78.

[3] Palmer, p. 78.

towards the "opposition," in addition to other issues, created conflicts between them that would mar their relationship until D.D.'s death in 1913.

Daniel David Palmer was a short, stocky man, with a cultivated bushy beard. He often wore a black, broad-brimmed western hat and drove around town in a buggy pulled by his matched team of horses. He loved his horses, and his favourites were called "Nip" and "Tuck"(which could be considered a metaphor for his own life).

In debate or discussion, he was an elegant and persuasive speaker, powerful in his opinions and unpredictable in his response. With his lawyer and friend Cornelius Murphy, Esq., Palmer successfully defended himself a number of times against prosecutors' charges that he was "illegally practising medicine." His success in these cases was important in order to establish the credibility of chiropractics. Eventually the prosecutors stopped making charges against him, and that led to the general peace that has prevailed between traditional medicine and chiropracty since then.

D.D. described himself as "the one who discovered the basic principle of chiropractic, developed its philosophy, originated and founded the science and art of correcting abnormal functions by hand adjusting, using the vertebral processes as levers."[4]

That Daniel David Palmer is little remembered in Canada today (except by the chiropractic profession, the Canada Memorial Chiropractic College, and the Town of Port Perry) is regrettable, because he made a significant contribution to his profession and, unquestionably, to millions of people around the world who have back problems.

[4] Dr. Paul Smallie. *Encyclopedia Chriopractica* (Stockton: World Wide Books, 1990), p. 13.

John Patch

Inventor: Screw Propeller for Ships

He was an inventor of exceptional talent and vision, and even his designs and devices incorporated and accommodated his knowledge and love of the sea.

In 1836, the British patent office issued patent #7104, for a marine screw propeller, to Francis Pettit-Smith, a farmer from Suffolk, England. Yet it is clear from existing records of the time that Yarmouth, Nova Scotia, shipwright and inventor John Patch had not only developed a practical design for a marine screw propeller in 1832, but also that he had built and tested it successfully — in front of many witnesses — in 1834, fully two years before it was "officially invented" by Pettit-Smith in 1836. Pettit-Smith received a knighthood and £6,000. John Patch died a pauper in the Yarmouth poorhouse. So murky was the world of invention in the nineteenth century that despite compelling evidence disputing ownership, inventions were often attributed to the wrong person. And while we tend to think of "trade secrets" and "corporate sabotage" as twentieth century phenomena, there are hints of such industrial espionage in John Patch's story. Like a tragic movie script, his life was a series of setbacks and misadventures.

John Patch was born in Nova Scotia, the son of sea captain Nehemiah Patch, who lost his life when his schooner *Polly* sank off Seal Island in 1871 — the year that John Patch was born.

Patch had many occupations in his early life, including that of a sailor, a fisherman, and a shipwright. His life was devoted to the sea. He was an inventor of exceptional talent and vision, and even his designs and devices incorporated and accommodated his knowledge and love of the sea.

In the new age of steamships, the propulsion of choice was the paddle wheel, which was known to use fuel inefficiently and to limit the potential speed the vessel could achieve. The screw propeller had always been one of the alternative possibilities for ship propulsion, but a practical design had not yet appeared. Certainly, the great Greek inventor Archimedes had proven the power of a helical screw to move water in 300 B.C. Archytos of Tarentum, another Greek inventor, is said to have invented a helical propeller for use on ships in 400 B.C., but there is no evidence of his design. In fact, although there had been other instances of propeller designs for marine propulsion earlier in the nineteenth century, they were not pursued for some reason.

However, the flurry of activity in the 1830s led to the first operational marine screw propeller, and John Patch was clearly in the forefront in designing what is considered to be one of the most significant technological advances in the industrial era. (Remember that the screw propeller was later successfully adapted for the power turbine, propeller-driven aircraft, and the jet engine.)

John Patch built his first propeller in his workshop in Kelley's Cove near Yarmouth, Nova Scotia, where he tested it in the harbour in 1833. Even though the hand-cranked fan-design propeller, mounted on a rowboat, achieved speeds of up to 6 knots, Patch was not satisfied with its performance and spent the next winter modifying and improving his design. The new model incorporated one complete turn of the screw. The propeller was mounted on a 7.6 metre (25-foot) shaft that could be secured beneath the waterline at the stern of a ship. A connecting windlass crank was linked to the deck, where it could be turned to operate the gears. The screw in the water was about 60 centimetres (two feet) in diameter. Records indicate that Patch was assisted in building his device by two other shipwrights, R.D. Butler and his brother Nathan, as well as Patch's best friend, Captain Silas Kelley.

In the summer of 1834, Patch and Captain Kelley were aboard the *Royal George*, Kelley's 25-ton schooner when "along with other vessels they were becalmed about 20 miles west of Saint John, New Brunswick. The screw was hoisted over the stern, secured, and the two men worked the crank. Suddenly, to the (surprise) of the crews on the other ships, the *Royal George* started to move forward with a steady speed for the harbour and left them far behind."[1] Captain Kelley was convinced that it was important for Patch to record his invention by obtaining a patent without delay, and he financed Patch's trip to the U.S. patent office in Washington, D.C.

Patch had a poor sense of business, and it would have been better for both men if Kelley (who had a keen sense of business) had accompanied him to Washington. When Patch arrived at the U.S. patent office, he was persuaded by the officials that his invention was silly, impractical, and of no particular value to anyone. So, he unwisely did not apply for a patent, even though no similar invention existed in the U.S. patent office files at the time. Clearly, someone with more business savvy would have recorded the invention at the patent office, regardless of the response. However, Patch had a lifetime motto of "time enough yet." These words he lived by contributed to his lack of official recognition for what was probably his pioneer work in marine mechanics.

When Patch returned to Yarmouth, Kelley urged him to go to England to obtain a patent there. And again, Kelley offered to pay all Patch's expenses. But Patch was in no hurry for he still believed there was "time enough yet."

Obviously, he was wrong! There was not time enough! Whether his design was stolen by two shipboard drinking companions on his trip to Washington, D.C., as he always contended, or whether the U.S. patent office officials hoodwinked him, it is clear that he told too many people about his invention without protecting it first, and thus, he did not receive the recognition he deserved.

However, undeterred, Patch continued working on other inventions, including improvements to the steam engine and the paddle wheel. He also developed an improved design for his own marine propeller, and this was recorded in an article about him that appeared in the highly respected journal *Scientific American*

[1] "Poor John Patch," *The Atlantic Advocate*, January 1978, p. 38.

in 1848. This improved design was the prototype of the one that eventually drove the great ocean steamship liners like the *Queen Mary* and the *Queen Elizabeth* in the twentieth century. But it too seems not to have been patented. John Patch clearly needed a business manager!

Patch did not understand that great inventions are not the end of the process, but just the beginning. If he had, the fruits of his inventive mind would have been better rewarded with wealth and fame. Instead, he died a pauper in the Yarmouth poorhouse, and even his own town council would not grant him a small pension for his accomplishments!

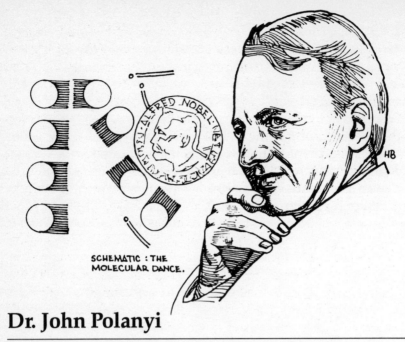

SCHEMATIC : THE
MOLECULAR DANCE.

Dr. John Polanyi

Research Scientist: Nobel Prize for Chemical Laser Research

The chemical laser is one of the late twentieth century's most exciting —
and potentially frightening — technological advances.

Attempting to explain the scientific revelation that earned
John Polanyi the Nobel Prize in Chemistry in 1986 would
be like trying to capture moonbeams in a bucket. In fact, Polanyi's
ideas were so obscure in 1960 when he first proposed them that
even the prestigious technical journal *Physical Review Letters*
turned down his paper because his theories seemed not to have
any scientific interest.

Interest indeed! In that same year, Polanyi resubmitted his
paper to the *Journal of Chemical Physics,* and it was promptly
published. The operational chemical lasers that were subsequently built were based on the research that he first put forward publicly in this paper. What was originally seen not to have
any scientific interest has led to one of the late twentieth century's
most exciting (and potentially frightening) technological advances: the chemical laser. ("Laser" is an acronym for *Light Am-
plification* by the *Stimulated Emission* of *Radiation.*)

No one really understands lasers except technical specialists like

John Polanyi himself (who probably cannot understand why we do not understand). The laser can do miraculous things: cut through diamond, the hardest substance known; cut and weld metals; direct its powerful beam onto the moon or at rockets in space. No other instrument can measure distance in space more accurately than the laser. New laser tools have been developed for use in surgery to seal arteries beneath the skin and to repair the retina. From compact discs to fibre optics, the laser's use in the communications industry seems almost endless. It holds untold potential for good in our world . . . and for evil. A military application of lasers in space as a "star war" technology is not inconceivable. However, it would contradict John Polanyi's own philosophical outlook: He is an avowed activist against nuclear weapons, particularly in space, and the use of "star war" technologies, including the military use of lasers. This is a common challenge facing scientists who design technological innovations or new concepts. They cannot always control the use and application of their work.

John Polanyi was born in 1929, in Berlin, Germany, where his father was a famous professor of chemistry. The family left Hitler's Germany in 1933, when John was only four years old. His father then became professor of chemistry at the University of Manchester in England. When John was 11 years old, he was sent to Canada, as were many other children in wartime Britain. He spent the war years with an "adopted" family in Toronto, Ontario, where John attended the University of Toronto School. When the war was over, he returned to Manchester to complete his education, earning a Ph.D. in chemistry from the University of Manchester. He was fortunate enough to attend his father's last classes in chemistry before his father, who had started his career as a physician, became a professor of philosophy at Manchester. John then moved back to Canada, where he did two years of post-graduate work with Ned Steacie and Gerhard Herzberg at the National Research Council. Polanyi then spent two years as a post-doctoral fellow at Princeton University in New York. He moved back to Toronto in 1956 when he was appointed as a lecturer in chemistry at the University of Toronto. He became a full professor of chemistry and remained there for the rest of his career where he carried out his research that led to his Nobel Prize.

In simple terms, Polanyi's research predicted that the light emission created in the process of a chemical reaction between hydrogen and chlorine might be used to create a laser. Lasers were not new! They had been predicted by Einstein as far back as 1917, and others had been developed in the late 1950s; however, a chemical laser had never been built.

For a non-scientist, it is very difficult to believe that you could get a molecule so excited in a chemical reaction that it would give off infrared radiation, and that if you could get enough of them doing so in a controlled way, you could create a laser. This was "chemiluminescence" as Polanyi technically called it, or the "molecular dance," which was his more poetic way of saying the same thing.

When Jerome Kaspar and George Pimentel built the first working chemical laser at Berkeley, California, in 1965, it was based on the principles outlined by Polanyi. They used the very same chemical reactions that he had proposed. These lasers are now among the most powerful and efficient in the world.[1]

In order to begin his research in the 1950s at the University of Toronto, Polanyi needed an "infrared spectrometer," which cost $10,000 (a considerable sum at the time). The Dean of Arts, Vincent Bladen, somehow found the money for Polanyi, but told him, "You better win a Nobel Prize with it!"[2]

John Polanyi shared the 1986 Nobel Prize in Chemistry with Dudley Herschbach of Harvard and with Yuan Lee of the University of California at Berkeley. Polanyi became the fifth Canadian to receive a Nobel Prize. On the very day he was given the prize, the Canadian government unwisely announced that it was cutting back the budget of the National Research Council by $20 million with the loss of 200 jobs. Ironically, the department where John Polanyi had worked when he began the research that led to his Nobel Prize was one of those most heavily hit. While he was thrilled to win the Nobel Prize, he was shocked by the insensitivity of the government. He used his new-found public status to denounce the government for savaging its universities and research institutes. "If we are neglecting our universities, we are neglecting thought. Surely, we can't allow ourselves to do that," he said.[3] Polanyi always enjoyed asking prospective sponsors of basic re-

[1] Lydia Dotto. *University of Toronto Alumni Magazine*, Winter 96, p. 10.

[2] Dotto, p. 10.

[3] Dotto, p. 11.

search if they would have been willing to gamble research money on the kind of theory he had proposed if there were no guarantee that it could eventually be turned into a major technology like the laser.

Not all Nobel Prize winners are well known publicly, but they are all well known in their scientific community. John Polanyi is both! Gerhard Herzberg, his old colleague and mentor at the National Research Council in Ottawa, called Polanyi "one of the top 10 physical chemists in the world."[4]

Polanyi is also Canada's most outspoken scientist. His clear, precise eloquence and his thoughtful intelligence make him a supremely positive image for the scientific community, and he is always a good "sound bite" for the media. He has even poked gentle fun at himself and his colleagues by commenting, "Scientists are supposed to wrap themselves in an envelope of obscurity, that's why we drone on when we give papers."[5]

He has spoken out continually in his new public fame, for causes that he feels passionately about, including the environment, disarmament, nuclear free outer space, star wars, and public funding for pure science. And he is particularly well equipped to do this because he is a knowledgeable and articulate speaker who can popularize the technical jargon in a way that it can be understood by average people. He is also a dignified, attractive, gracious, and personable man.

In 1994, Stephen Strauss, the science reporter for the *Globe and Mail*, asked Polanyi if he had any regrets in his life. Polanyi said no . . . then on reflection, he added, "Of course, I would have liked to do the same things, but much better."[6]

[4] Judy Steed. "A Crusader . . . ," *The Globe and Mail*, June 6, 1982.
[5] Joanne Strong. "The Informal . . . " *The Globe and Mail*, August 10, 1982.
[6] Stephen Strauss. "A Chemist . . ." *The Globe and Mail*, November 3, 1994.

Charles Saunders

Research Scientist and Inventor: Development of Marquis Wheat

Charles sifted through the shafts of wheat, testing each one individually by his chewing method. He selected only the grains on those shafts that came up to his rigid standards.

It has been said of Charles Saunders that he made Canada a major player in world wheat production, and there is a grain of truth to that! By developing the hardy, robust, full-bodied "Marquis" strain of wheat with its relatively short growing season, Charles Saunders developed a wheat that was ideally suited to the climate of the Canadian prairies and other northern grain-growing regions of the world. This made him one of the most successful scientists in developing grains adaptable to the environments in which they would be grown. Although he was a world giant in biological engineering, Charles Saunders was really a shy, retiring, frail, and self-effacing man, who at one time in his life taught music and wrote poetry.

His father was an immigrant from England, who came to Canada at the age of 12. He was first employed in a drug store in London, Ontario. By the time he was 20, he owned the drug store, and by the time he was 30, he was a professor of pharmacy at the

University of Western Ontario. When Charles was only a year old, the family moved to a farm outside London, where his father could indulge his passions for horticulture and entomology (the study of insects). He turned his farm into a mini experimental farm and a "classroom" in biology for his daughter and five sons. While Charles seemed to share his father's passions to some degree, he had other interests he wanted to pursue as well. However, Charles' dominant father recognized his son's horticultural talent and steered him inexorably in that direction.

After graduating from the University of Toronto, Charles received a scholarship to Johns Hopkins University in Baltimore, Maryland, where he earned a Ph.D. in chemistry in 1891. He was then appointed professor of chemistry at the University of Kentucky, where he served for one year and then decided he was not cut out to be a teacher.

By this time, the Canadian federal government had asked Charles' father to draw up plans for a national experimental farm — along the lines of his own farm, but on a much grander scale. He not only did that, but also gave up pharmacy and accepted the position of first Director of the Experimental Farm in Ottawa, and moved his family there.

Charles and his brother Percy spent their summers working on the experimental farm, helping their father in his work and learning the trade. Charles rebelled briefly, in a modest way by taking a teaching post as music instructor at Havergal Ladies College in Toronto, where he could practise his singing, play his flute, study French, and write poetry. He also served as the music critic for the *Toronto Globe* newspaper (which later merged with the *Toronto Mail and Empire* to become the *Toronto Globe and Mail*). During this period of his life in Toronto, Charles met and married Mary Blackwell, a beautiful and brilliant young soprano, who was already modestly famous for her voice. But Charles also remained close to his family, and finally succumbed to his father's appeals to join him permanently on the experimental farm.

In 1903, Charles became the "experimentalist" in the cereals department of the experimental farm. In 1905, the title was changed to "cerealist," and finally to "Dominion cerealist," the title he held until his retirement in 1922. It was a very grand title, but he was in fact the *only* cerealist. As well, it was a new position established by the director of the federal experimental farm — his father. But it was a good decision. As Charles himself acknowledged, he was a scientist who had been trained all his life for this particular role, and no one was better qualified.

In 1881, 65,000 people lived in western Canada. With the completion of the transcontinental Canadian Pacific Railway in 1886, and with cheap new land suddenly available, thousands of prospective farmers flooded west, bringing their eastern Canadian and European farming techniques and practices with them. By 1901, the 65,000 people in western Canada had grown to almost half a million, with farming as their major focus. It very soon became clear that "Red Fife," the standard wheat variety commonly in use in Ontario, had a growing season that was too long for the shorter western summer, leaving it vulnerable to early frost. The farmers who watched their crops grow to maturity were devastated when early frost destroyed them. The farmers urged the federal government to produce a wheat variety with the same high quality as Red Fife, but with a shorter growing season.

Between 1885 and 1897, using seed from around the world, especially from regions with climates similar to that of the prairies, the experimental farm developed and tested over 700 new varieties of wheat. None was exactly what the researchers wanted. Although the search began in 1885, and went on for years, it was not until Charles joined them that the researchers began to apply sophisticated scientific techniques to the selection process. But it was still two parts science and one part inspiration. Charles included some unique and unconventional approaches in his testing process. Not only did he test the normal features of the grain and its growing period, he also tested its milling qualities, and even baked the flour into small loaves to see what quality of bread it produced. He also personally chewed every new variety of grain that was developed, to test its gluten quality (or its ability to hold together in a pulped state). While none of the new grains had both the quality of Red Fife *and* a shorter growing season — one did show promise. It had been called Markham and was a cross pollination of Red Fife and Hard Red Calcutta. It had been produced by Percy Saunders in 1892 and then set aside. The shorter growing season was right, but the quality was not consistent. Charles sifted through the shafts of wheat, testing each one individually by his chewing method. He selected only the grains on those shafts that came up to his rigid standards. By starting with

100

only a few shafts, it was a slow process to create enough seed grain to test. But in 1906, working with Angus McKay, a farmer from Saskatchewan, Charles Saunders had finally gathered enough seed for limited distribution.

Since he thought "Markham" not quite "regal" enough for the name of his new strain of wheat, he called it "Marquis." The rest, as they say, is history! Except for one small detour. The original precious experimental seed was stolen from Angus McKay's farm. Years of work would have to be re-done if the seed grain was not recovered. They immediately advised the public of the significance of this theft and of the devastating effect it could have on the prospects for future wheat harvest in the prairies. The stolen seed grain was returned anonymously the next day. Could you imagine that happening today?

"Marquis" wheat was an immediate success. In its first crop year, it matured a full week to ten days earlier than Red Fife and it produced five bushels to the acre more than Red Fife. Its spikes stood up firmly for harvesting and it had all the other qualities necessary to satisfy Charles Saunders' rigorous standards. Marquis seed was available in quantity by the 1910 crop year, and by 1920, fully 90% of the Canadian wheat crop was Marquis. In 1911, at the World's Fair in New York, Marquis wheat was awarded the gold prize as the best wheat grown anywhere in the world. By 1912, the Canadian Parliament had passed the Canada Grain Act, which used Marquis wheat as the standard grading of excellence against which all other wheat was measured. Soon Marquis was in use all over the world in places where quality and a short growing season were important. Awards and recognition continued to be heaped on this remarkably successful grain. While Charles Saunders continued to work on other cereal grain research, the major new setback was the spread of wheat rust, a parasitic blight that affected the wheat crop. The challenge was to develop a rust resistant strain that would protect the crop production. Having produced the Marquis strain, Charles Saunders was now instrumental in producing Ruby, Garnet, and Reward. He developed these successful new varieties, using the same rigid selection process that had brought him his first great success.

He was made a fellow of the Royal Society of Canada in 1921, and received the Flavelle Medal of the Society in 1923. In 1922, his health broke down, and he was forced to retire from the experimental farm. While he had been instrumental in making Canada "the bread basket of the world" — generating billions of dollars for the Canadian economy and the Canadian food industry — he received no special monetary recognition or reward from those he had helped to enrich. Indeed, there was not even provision for a pension for someone who was forced to retire early from ill health. Charles Saunders was left almost destitute until a special appeal was made on his behalf by an Ottawa newspaper. This moved the federal government to grant Saunders a lifetime pension, which greatly eased his financial distress.

In his retirement he spent three years at the Sorbonne in Paris, France, studying French literature, which had been a lifelong interest for him. On his return to Canada, he published a book of his own poetry, written in French and called *Essais de Vers*.

In 1933, Charles Saunders was knighted by King George V for his contribution to world agriculture. But he was quick to point out that while he was the formal recipient, the honour was shared with his colleagues, including his brother Percy, his father William, and his associate Will Macoun. Their early research and developmental work had solved enough of the puzzle that Charles was able to add the last piece of the puzzle.

His gentle wife died in 1936, and shortly afterwards, this shy scientist, who treasured his privacy and nurtured other dreams, also passed away. But he is remembered today as the man who — along with those who built the railway — helped to open up the west to the development of a new society; and as the man who made Canada one of the leading wheat producers in the world!

Sir William Stephenson

Research Scientist and Inventor: Transmission of Photographs by Radio Waves

He was a war hero, an ace pilot, a world-calibre boxer, a spy. . . and an ingenious inventor, whose most famous invention helped revolutionize the modern communications field.

Roger Moore, a British actor who played James Bond in the movies was once asked at a press conference in Winnipeg, Manitoba, if he knew who Sir William Stephenson was. He said, "Of course! He was a spy." But he was much more than that. Sir William Stephenson was one of those shadowy figures who, in wartime Britain, lurked on the edges of history, doing what spies normally do: steal secrets, break codes, mislead the enemy, carry out industrial and political espionage, and generally risk their lives to find out enemy plans. And they try to remain invisible!

In World War II, Stephenson was one of Britain's master spies, and was assigned by Churchill to set up Britain's counter-intelligence network in America in the event that Hitler was able to defeat Britain. "Spies" generally shunned publicity and the glare of public scrutiny, but Stephenson's story slowly emerged over the decades that followed World War II, and it is truly the stuff of great adventure. His exploits and his contribution to the war effort were eventually recognized by the Queen, who knighted him in 1962. Stephenson was a man of genius, who did many things well and lived his life to the fullest.

At this point you might ask, "What is one of Britain's master spies doing in a book about Canadian inventors?" Well, Stephenson *was* a Canadian, and he was also a brilliant inventor, in addition to all the other things he did so well. His most famous invention, the wireless photograph transmission system, helped to revolutionize the modern communications field.

He was born in 1896 and grew up in Point Douglas near Winnipeg, where his great childhood passions were books, electronics, mathematics, and boxing. He was in high school when World War I broke out, and he promptly enlisted. From then on, his life seemed just like a script from an adventure movie.

After a brief training period, he was sent to the war front in France with the Royal Canadian Engineers, which was almost considered a death sentence. Young soldiers were used as little more than cannon fodder by uncaring generals and inept politicians who did not know first-hand the full horror of "trench warfare." So many of the officers and soldiers around him were killed or wounded that by elimination Stephenson received a field commission as a lieutenant and was promoted to captain on his exceptional merit before he was 20 years old. In his 20 months at the front he was gassed twice. After the second gas poisoning, he was sent back to England to recover, but his doctors declared that his lungs were too damaged to allow him to return to the front to fight in the ground offensive. Thwarted on the ground, he transferred to the air corps, where he served with great distinction until the end of the war.

During this period, he shot down "26 enemy planes,"[1] including a "force down" of the "Red Baron's" brother Lothar von Richthofen. Near the end of the war, he was shot down himself by what the Americans now call "friendly fire," but which was known then as being "shot down by mistake by your own side." He was wounded and imprisoned for three months by the Germans. One month before the war ended, he escaped and returned to his own side in time to take part in the victory celebration. By war's end,

[1] William Stevenson. *A Man Called Intrepid: The Secret War* (New York/London: Harcourt, Brace, Jovanovich, 1976), p 10.

he was a famous air ace and a flight commander. He received the distinguished Flying Cross, the Military Cross, the French Legion of Honour and the Croix de Guerre with Palm. A very distinguished military career for one so young. He was only 22 years old, but he had lived a lifetime. As he said to one of his colleagues, "every day beyond my twentieth birthday, I consider to be a bonus."[2]

He was extremely proud that he "became the interservice lightweight boxing champion on the same program that Gene Tunney became the heavyweight champion."[3] They remained lifetime friends. Gene Tunney went on to be Heavyweight Boxing Champion of the World.

After a brief stay at Oxford, where he studied aeronautical engineering and radio communications, Stephenson returned to Winnipeg and taught math and science at the University of Manitoba. But he was restless, and when he was called back by Admiral Hall, Britain's master spy of the time, to work in the emerging field of "cryptanalysis" (electronics, codes, and communication), he was only too eager to comply. The timing was perfect for Stephenson.

With the creation of the British Broadcasting Corporation in 1921, radio became available to everyone for the first time, and opened a new dimension to information and communication systems. Based on the invention of Canadian Reginald Fessenden, the new technology made fortunes for those who moved quickly into the manufacture of home receiving sets or radios. Stephenson was one of those early entrepreneurs, and in addition to manufacturing thousands of radios, his labs also explored the many emerging opportunities in the electronic world. He wrote a paper on "Television" in 1923. He also worked on the conversion of light variations into radio waves and then into electric current to transmit photographs. His work in this field was backed by his friend Lord Northcliffe, the owner of the *London Daily Mail*. Stephenson's breakthrough was his invention of the first workable telephoto transmission system, which he had worked on initially at the University of Manitoba in 1921, but perfected and patented in England in 1922.

---

[2] Stevenson, p. 14.
[3] Stevenson, p. 10.

Stevenson's system was based on a photo-electric scanning process whereby the whole photo was translated into light dots of various intensity, which corresponded to the light, shade, or shadow on the photograph. These dots in turn were converted into electrical impulses that could be transmitted by radio or telephone. A receiver at the other end converted these electrical impulses through a reversal of the process to recreate an image of the original photograph. Stephenson used an ingenious method of tandem, rotating discs with radial slits in them to scan the photograph effectively, which gave him a reconstituted photograph of great integrity and high quality.

In December 1922, Lord Northcliffe's *London Daily Mail* newspaper transmitted and converted into print the first photograph by radio. It was an instant success and a defining moment in the world of communications. All the major newspapers throughout the world adopted this system almost immediately. As a result, Stephenson became a millionaire by the time he was 30 years old, and he continued to work on the development of new electronic technologies in his labs and to extend his industrial empire.

When World War II was imminent, his old colleagues from the previous war years were emerging in positions of power in Churchill's government-in-waiting. And William Stephenson was included on the team. He was eventually appointed by Churchill to work under the code name "Intrepid" to set up Britain's spy network. Churchill told Stephenson that he wanted him to direct Britain's Secret Intelligence Service from New York in the event that Britain was invaded by Germany, and that Stephenson was to be Churchill's personal link to President Roosevelt. The New York operation was called British Security Co-ordination with Stephenson as its director. It operated publicly as a British passport office in Rockefeller Center. At one point in the war, Stephenson effectively controlled all four major British Intelligence departments, including MI-5. He set up a secondary centre in Hamilton, Bermuda. He also established the "mysterious" spy school "Camp X" in Oshawa, Ontario, where field agents received their basic training and where major operations were planned. Reputed to be among the spy school's more illustrious alumni were Noel Coward, Graham Greene, Cary Grant, David Niven, Vivian Leigh, Lester Pearson, and Ian Fleming. It was also rumoured in the secretive world of spies that other famous couriers who may have visited the Oshawa spy school included Guy Burgess and Donald Maclean.[4] Ian Fleming went on to create the James Bond novels, and it has been suggested that Sir William Stephenson was the prototype for "M," the master spy in the Bond series.

Sir William Stephenson retired to New York, and then like some other prominent Canadians, moved to Bermuda, where he lived until his death in 1989.

In a famous photograph from the war, a brooding Churchill is seen inspecting the rubble in front of the Parliament Buildings after a particularly destructive bombing raid on London, and he is accompanied by a "shadowy" figure whose back is to the camera. That shadowy figure was Sir William Stephenson. As he has slowly emerged from the "shadows" through excellent biographies, novels, and the revelations of famous former "spy students," an interesting phenomenon has developed. There are now "William Stephenson" clubs (like Sherlock Holmes clubs) in a number of cities, including Stephenson's home town of Winnipeg. However, unlike Sherlock Holmes, William Stephenson really *did* exist!

So the next time you use your television or fax machine think of Sir William Stephenson and his pioneer work in developing the precursors of these modern machines that most of us today believe we could not possibly live without.

---

[4] Burgess and Maclean were senior officers in the British Intelligence Service during the war and after. They were revealed as Russian spies when they defected to Russia in the 1950s.

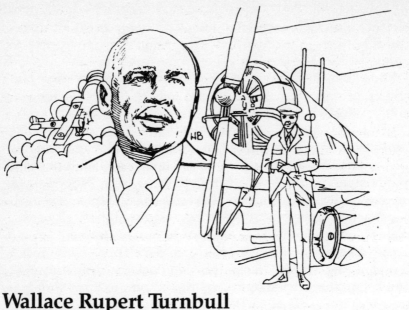

Wallace Rupert Turnbull

Inventor and Aircraft Pioneer

Turnbull's wife thought it best that he keep the nature of his experiments as quiet as possible. She did not want him to appear to be a flying machine "crank," of which there were many at the time.

When you enter the National Aviation Museum in Ottawa, the whole history of Canadian aviation is presented to you under one massive roof in this modern, bright, and airy space. It is one of Canada's undiscovered treasures. All the major air milestones along the way are highlighted by the aircraft and all the associated Canadians who have made significant contributions to our twentieth century adventure with flight. The Avro *Arrow* is there, of course — or at least small bits of it; Alexander Graham Bell's *Silver Dart*, the first Canadian-built plane to fly in Canada; *Lancasters, Spitfires,* and *Messerschmitts* from World War II . . . And much, much more!

It is a progression of the dreams of successive generations of Canadian air pioneers who, each in their own way, added an element or more to our collective knowledge of flight.

Occupying a special place of honour and prominence in one of the first exhibits is Wallace Rupert Turnbull, a Canadian aeronautical engineer. In 1927, he successfully tested his variable pitch propeller on an Avro *504K* biplane at Camp Borden airbase, thereby ushering in the new age of commercial flight, which had not been possible before.

What is the variable pitch propeller, and why was it important? Well, think of it in terms of how you operate a car. You start your car in low gear to get it moving; you move it to second gear to accelerate the speed; and finally, you move it to cruising speed, where the car can be driven comfortably without straining the engine. The variable pitch propeller does essentially the same thing for a propeller-driven airplane. It changes the angle, or pitch, that the propeller blade slices through the air. With Turnbull's propeller, pilots could control the angle of the propeller blade for maximum efficiency at all engine speeds. Maximum pitch for push to get the plane started and airborne, and progressively less pitch as it reaches cruising speed and altitude. Turnbull's device, which was controlled by a small electric motor, provided aircraft with faster take-off, rapid climb, increased altitude, better cruise control, and improved fuel consumption. His propeller also made it possible to carry more passengers and heavier cargo more safely, regardless of engine speed. Overcoming these obstacles made the great age of commercial air transport possible. At the time, it was considered to be the most important advance in the history of aircraft and "as essential to aviation as the gearbox is to the automobile."[1]

Wallace Rupert Turnbull was born in 1870, in Rothesay, New Brunswick, on the outskirts of St. John. He graduated in engineering from Cornell University at Ithaca, New York, and did postgraduate work in Berlin and Heidelberg in Germany.

Like many other brilliant young inventors of the time, Turnbull found employment and training opportunities at Thomas Edison's lamp factory in Harrison, New Jersey. Hired as an experimental engineer, he worked there for six years, but was forced to leave in 1905 because of ill health. He returned to Rothesay, where he established his own engineering office and created his own laboratory in a barn adjacent to his property. Except for a brief period during World War I, Turnbull remained there for the rest of

---

[1] Donald J.C. Phillipson. "Wallace Rupert Turnbull," *The Canadian Encyclopedia* (Edmonton: Hurtig Publishers, 1988), p. 2022.

his life and carried out most of his experimental work in his constantly expanding laboratory.

His early work was devoted almost exclusively to aeronautics. That he was a true pioneer in this field is obvious when you realize that in 1901 Orville and Wilbur Wright had not yet made their first successful airplane flight. (In fact, that event did not occur until December 17, 1903.) So when Turnbull started down the path of his own aircraft experiments, the means of flight and propulsion that would ultimately be used was not at all clear because it had not yet been done. However, Turnbull had already decided that the airplane would soon be a reality and that its means of propulsion would be an engine-driven propeller.

Turnbull's wife thought it best that he keep the nature of his experiments as quiet as possible. She did not want him to appear to be "a flying machine crank,"[2] of which there were many at the time.

In 1902, in order to test his theories of propulsion and aerodynamics, Turnbull built Canada's first wind tunnel in his workshop. In everything, he was meticulous, thorough, and painstakingly committed to exactness and detail. He kept clear, concise notes on all his experimental work and used them to thoroughly work out the practical application of his ideas. He studied the flight of birds, the conformation of their wings, and their air surfaces. This led him to test the aerodynamics of various forms of airfoils, and he subsequently patented a double curvature airfoil in 1906. "He considered the design of early aeroplanes were at best crude . . . and a series of compromises at every point."[3] He pointed out that inefficient wings meant larger propellers, inefficient propellers meant larger engines, larger engines meant larger planes and so on . . . ."[4] The whole process had to be made more efficient, and he believed that more and better research needed to be done on all aspects of flight.

He was one of the world's first aeronautical engineers, and while Rothesay may have seemed isolated from the great air pioneers of the age, Turnbull remained well connected to all of them. He earned their recognition and respect, including that of Alexander Graham Bell, who was just down the road at Baddeck,

[2] J.H. Parkin. *Canadian Aeronautical Journal*, January/February 1956, p. 4.
[3] Parkin, p. 7.
[4] Parkin, p. 7.

Nova Scotia. In 1908, long before his great invention, Turnbull was asked to read a paper on *The Efficiency of Aeroplanes, Propellers and Motors* at the Aeronautical Society of Great Britain. In a subsequent article in their journal, he wrote *The Efficiency of Aerial Propellers*, which earned him the Aeronautical Society's medal for the best article about aeronautics in their journal that year.

During World War I, Turnbull wanted to contribute to the war effort, and he eventually did so by working for Frederick Sage and Company in Peterborough, England. They had been commissioned by the British government to manufacture aircraft. Turnbull worked there first as an inspector, then as a designer. It was there that he first worked out the principles of his variable pitch propeller. He had even signed a tentative contract with the British government to develop it, but the war ended and the contract was cancelled. Governments do that sort of thing!

He took out patents on his invention when he returned to Canada after the war. Two years after the successful test flight in 1927, he sold his patent rights to the Curtis-Wright Aircraft Corporation in the United States for a cash settlement and royalty rights that assured him a continuing income in the years to come. Turnbull was primarily an aeronautical engineer, but in his lifetime he worked on many other engineering challenges, including bomb sights, torpedo screens, hydroplanes, and the harnessing of tidal waters for hydro-electric energy. This latter venture was something that had also occupied his mind for most of his life. At the time of his death in 1954, he was working on a project to harness the power of the tides in the Bay of Fundy.

Along with Reginald Fessenden, Thomas "Carbide" Willson, and Alexander Graham Bell, Turnbull was among the most prolific and successful of Canadian inventors. He is also considered to be the father of aeronautical engineering in Canada. He was greatly honoured in Britain (and more recently in Canada) for his exceptional contribution to the development of aircraft.

Everything Turnbull did, he did with gusto. In all his affairs, he was meticulous in the extreme. He was the best at everything that he could be. But, just to show that he was not all work, "he and his partner won the mixed doubles championship of an all-Canadian tennis tournament in 1910."[5] As indicated by the many trophies

[5] Parkin, p. 46.

he won, tennis remained a passion throughout his life. "An opponent after a trying game with him on the courts was heard to say that the particularly troublesome Turnbull strokes were undoubtedly the product of scientific laboratory research."[6]

Somehow it seems fitting that the St. John airport, which is situated in Rothesay, is named after its famous son Wallace Rupert Turnbull. And the famous propeller? It and an Avro 504K (on which it was successfully tested) are both on display at the National Aviation Museum in Ottawa, just down the street from the houses of the Prime Minister and the Governor General of Canada.

---

[6] Parkin, p. 46.

Joseph Burr Tyrrell

Pioneer and Land Surveyor: Discovered Dinosaurs Bones in Alberta

The Royal Tyrrell Museum is home to one of the world's largest displays of dinosaur fossils and is one of the world's great centres of research in paleontology.

In today's world, nurtured on monster movies, *Jurassic Park*, horror pulp novels, and Stephen Spielberg, dinosaurs are very real to us — even though they have been extinct for 65 million years! More specifically, the kind of dinosaur most commonly depicted is the famous *Tyrannosaurus rex*, which translated means "king of giant lizards." At 15 metres in length, and over 6 metres in height, the *Tyrannosaurus rex* was the world's largest-ever carnivore and would certainly terrify any reasonable person.

However, everything we know about dinosaurs today has been learned in just the last 150 years. Before that, we did not know that dinosaurs had even existed. While the first finds of dinosaur remains were made in southern England, others have since been found in almost every part of the world. As a result, a whole new field of scientific study — called paleontology — has opened up, and has vastly increased our knowledge of what dinosaurs looked like, the variety of different species, their habitats, their feeding habits, their social behaviours, and their evolutionary processes. We even have names for the various periods in which they existed. But how did they get to where their remains have been found? Why did they seem to disappear so suddenly? Which, if any, of today's modern animals are the dinosaurs' descendants? Were dinosaurs warm-blooded or cold-blooded? These are some of the questions that still confound the dinosaur experts today.

One of those experts is Philip Currie, a world-renowned paleontologist from the Royal Tyrrell Museum at Drumheller, Alberta. While the Royal Tyrrell Museum is not one of the wonders of the world, it should be! It is home to one of the world's largest displays of dinosaur fossils and is one of the world's great centres of research in paleontology. An outstanding institution, the Royal Tyrrell Museum is a place that all Canadians should try to visit at least once in their lifetime.

Why is the museum at Drumheller, and why is it called the Tyrrell Museum? Drumheller lies along the Red Deer River, in a vast area known as the Badlands of Alberta. Drumheller and the Badlands comprise one of the world's greatest sites of dinosaur remains. The first person to discover the Drumheller dinosaur beds was the Canadian geologist and explorer Joseph Burr Tyrrell. His encounter with the dinosaurs is like something out of a fantasy movie and is truly stranger than fiction. In the latter part of the nineteenth century, Tyrrell was employed with the "adventurers" in the Geological Survey of Western Canada. Like other great adventurers, Tyrrell wore many hats. He was a scientist, explorer, adventurer, sharpshooter, geologist, mining promoter, business-man, historian, and writer. Truly a man for all seasons!

Joseph Burr Tyrrell was born in 1858 and was raised in Weston, Ontario, which is now part of the Greater Toronto Area. But in Tyrrell's day, Weston was a thriving farming community, a place where a young boy could explore the woods and streams that still existed then. His father was from the Irish gentry and was very proud of his roots. He served as Reeve of Weston and was politically well connected. In addition, the senior Tyrrell had close associations to the Conservative party, because he had been an unsccessful political candidate several times.

Joseph Burr Tyrrell was educated at Upper Canada College and the University of Toronto. He never forgot his elite background. He was encouraged to enter the legal profession, but after a brief period in a law firm, he knew it wasn't for him. He wanted to work in the outdoors. With the help of his father's political connections, he succeeded in being assigned to the Geological Survey, a government agency whose work involved searching out mineral deposits and surveying and mapping the new territories of Canada.

For the first year-and-a-half, Tyrrell worked in the Ottawa headquarters, cataloguing the Geological Society's collection of fossils. He was not happy with this state of affairs and persisted in his attempts to get a field assignment. In 1883, he was most fortunate to be appointed to work with George Dawson, one of Canada's greatest exploration geologists. Tyrrell's first field assignment was very pedestrian — literally. He was given the task of making a "pace survey" of the journey over the Crow's Nest Pass through the Rocky Mountains. The pace survey consisted of walking over the pass and actually counting the steps between check points. In this great empty land, there were many dangers, including difficult climbing conditions, raging torrents, and even grizzly bears. There were also bandits in Canada's wild west, although they were generally tamed by the Royal Northwest Mounted Police. But even the police had their horses run off once at Fort McLeod and were decidedly "unmounted" at the time. At the end of the summer, Tyrrell returned to Ottawa to report his findings and prepare for the next year.

Under normal circumstances, Tyrrell would not have been given leadership of a survey team for several years. But with the rapid extension of the Canadian Pacific Railway westward, there was political pressure to find coal deposits to feed the railway along its route, and every capable man was pressed into service to lead a team. Dawson thought that Tyrrell was ready.

Tyrrell was assigned a vast region of what is now south central Alberta — an area roughly 72,000 square kilometres, extending north from Calgary to Edmonton, and east to what is now the Saskatchewan border. It was the normal practice of the geologists to travel by horseback, so much so that they were often called the "Geological Cavalry"! One of Tyrrell's strengths was his ability to adapt to situations. Since the Red Deer River ran through much of his territory, he decided early on to make a preliminary survey of the river and wisely chose to travel by canoe with his small party. As a now-seasoned geologist, he knew that where a river had carved its way into a valley, the valley walls would display the strata of earlier ages and would clearly reveal the mineral deposits.

On June 9, 1884, after paddling all morning, they stopped on the shore for lunch. As was Tyrrell's normal practice, he set off on foot after lunch to explore the river bank. At one point, he looked up the steep bank, where he noticed a large amber-coloured "something" protruding from the valley wall far above him. He clambered up and stared in disbelief at what he had found.

Tyrrell had stumbled upon the fossilized skeleton of a dinosaur in a region where they had not been found before. It would eventually prove to be the single largest find of dinosaur bones in North America! Later in that same month, Tyrrell was scrambling along a rock face on the valley wall, and as he turned a corner, he was shocked to see a monstrous head jutting out of the cliffside. With its rows of sabre teeth and large sightless eyes, it was a vision out of a nightmare. He knew for certain that nothing like it had ever been found before. This find alone should have justified the value of the trip, but he and Dawson both knew that to satisfy their political masters, they had to find natural resources — specifically, coal for the railway.

Tyrrell seemed to live under a lucky star, and he knew it. Three days after discovering the dinosaur graveyard, he continued along the river by canoe, and his luck came through again. He found evidence of a coal seam on the valley wall; and on further exploration, he found the outcropping of one of Canada's largest coal deposits. A discovery guaranteed to satisfy the politicians, to strengthen the position of the Geological Survey, and to establish his own reputation. Both of these finds were made in the area known as Alberta's Badlands, near present-day Drumheller.

At that time, there was no one in Canada who could evaluate Tyrrell's dinosaur bones, so they were sent to the Philadelphia Academy of Science, where, Professor Cape identified the dinosaur as a somewhat smaller member of the same family as *Tyrannosaurus rex*, and he named it *Albertosaurus*.[1]

Tyrrell spent three summers in the region carrying out his

[1] Renie Gross. *Dinosaur Country* (Saskatoon: Western Producer Prairie Books, 1985), p. 84.

surveys. Among his other significant finds were pools of black sticky surface oil near Edmonton. These deposits were duly recorded in his journals.

In 1893, the Geological Survey next sent Joe Tyrrell out to explore the vast uncharted territories west of Hudson's Bay and north of the treeline. When he began this trip, the area was generally a total mystery to everyone except the natives who lived there, and Sam Hearne, who had explored the region over 100 years before for the Hudson's Bay Company. Fortunately, Tyrrell read the maps and journals of Hearne and had some knowledge of what to expect. But nothing in a book could prepare him for the hardships and danger that he faced. On his first trip, his party almost starved to death; in fact they would have if Tyrrell had not been an exceptional marksman. He shot their food, including a polar bear. The expedition was three months overdue, and everyone had already given them up for lost when they finally arrived at West Selkirk. Tyrrell and his team had accomplished a Herculean feat of exploration that lifted some of the mystery from the far north and made Joe Tyrrell famous as one of the world's great explorers of the time.

Tyrrell stayed on with the Geological Survey until 1898, and continued to do important work until then. When he left, he became a geological consultant and worked at a number of different sites. He eventually became involved in the development of a gold mine in Kirkland Lake in northern Ontario. He became the president and general manager of this gold mine when he was 65. He lived to be 99 years old and stayed involved in his mining, as well as other pursuits, right to the end.

Tyrrell was famous in his day for his great adventures and discoveries. He was also greatly honoured in his own time. In 1947, London's Royal Geophysical Society awarded Joseph Tyrrell the rarely given Wollaston Palladium Medal. Previous distinguished recipients included such pioneers as Charles Darwin and Thomas Huxley.

Tyrrell might have been forgotten — his work buried like the bones he found. But thanks largely to the Royal Tyrrell Museum, which bears his name and feeds our incredible fascination with dinosaurs, Joseph Tyrrell will be remembered for his links to Canada's first dinosaur finds, and for that incredible week of discovery in June 1884. Enough to guarantee his official fame in textbooks if not popular fame like Wayne Gretzky.

James Miller Williams

Inventor and Pioneer: Developed World's First Drilled Oil Well

In our world, oil is power, and the oil industry is vastly more powerful than many governments. Our machine-driven society could not exist without it.

J ames Miller Williams was one of those people who personified a quirk in the Canadian psyche: We seldom honour our own heroes and pioneers . . . unless of course, they are honoured somewhere else first! James Miller Williams is a typical example.

The British government recognized and honoured him as the discoverer of petroleum and as the producer of the best manufactured oils. In the U.S. geological records, maintained in Washington, D.C., Williams is identified as "the discoverer of petroleum and the pioneer in its refinement and preparation for illuminating and lubricating purposes."[1] In addition, Williams was the first major exporter of oil. All this placed him at the very beginning of one of the world's great industries, and at the introduction of a product that has changed the world.   Petroleum — oil — has

---

[1] Hope Morrit. *Rivers of Oil: The Founding of America's Petroleum Industry* (Kingston: Quarry Press, 1993) p. 31.

been at the centre of wars. It has toppled governments, deposed kings, created empires, and changed the map of the world. It is often referred to as "black gold," and it is more assiduously sought after than either diamonds or precious metals. Oil has provided vast wealth to those who have it or who control it. Those without it, want it. In our world, oil is power, and the oil industry is vastly more powerful than many governments. Our machine-driven society could not exist without it. And it was Williams, a Canadian, who first drilled for it, refined it, and exported it from the site that is now called Oil Springs, Ontario, located near aptly named Petrolia and the city of Sarnia, which today is a major Canadian oil refining centre. But few Canadians outside of the oil industry know anything about Williams.

James Miller Williams was born in Camden, New Jersey, shortly after the War of 1812. Many American families, including the Williams family, came from British roots and fostered a sense of attachment to British values. Williams was apprenticed as a teenager to a Camden carriage maker from whom he learned a very marketable trade. Apparently, by the time Miller was 22 years old, his parents were already dead. With nothing to keep him in Camden, he decided to leave the United States and move to British North America. And in North America, what could be more British than London, Ontario? So in 1840, he set off for London, Ontario, to seek work there as a carriage maker. He brought along his sister and the remains of his dead baby brother. Travelling with the remains of his dead brother was one of the more bizarre aspects of his life, but not the only unusual one!

In 1842, he married another American-born Canadian, Melinda Jackson, and they moved to Hamilton, Ontario, in 1846. He joined H.G. Cooper as co-owner of the Hamilton Coach Factory, which was re-named the Williams and Cooper Carriage Factory within a year. They were very successful, particularly in manufacturing railway cars for the new Great Western Railway that travelled from Toronto through Hamilton and London, on its way to Detroit. Williams was not only a successful businessman, but also a local politician who had already served two terms as an alderman in Hamilton by 1855. It was therefore somewhat surprising that he would suddenly give up a thriving and successful career for a new and speculative adventure in an industry that did not yet exist. But that is exactly what Williams did.

He believed that oil was the fuel of the future, and that there was great potential for discovering oil in Enniskillen Township, northwest of London, Ontario. He based his belief on survey reports that were done in the early 1850s by Alexander Murray, which indicated the presence of surface oil and asphalt on land owned by Henry Tripp in the same district.

Williams tried his first wells at Bothwell, and then relocated his operation to land near Oil Springs, Ontario. After many unsuccessful attempts, he eventually brought in the world's first oil well, in August of 1858. *The Sarnia Observer Advertiser* of August 5, 1858, announced that "an important discovery has just been made in the township of Enniskillen . . . a party digging a well at the edge of a bed of Bitumen struck upon a vein of oil . . . ."[2] Williams' well produced five to 100 barrels of black oil a day, which he then refined through a heat distillation process that produced an oil with a clear amber colour. Unfortunately, his distilled oil had the foul smell of sulphur, and for years it was called "skunk juice"! Nevertheless, the news of his discovery spread quickly, and it did not take long before all the oil speculators, camp followers, and the "get-rich-quick" crowd had descended on him. All around him, wells were being dug in a quagmire of mud and confusion. But Williams had wisely bought up tracts of land around his find, and so was able to proceed relatively unobstructed.

One of his main problems was shipping his oil to market. Although it could be shipped by train from the rail connection at Wyoming 24 kilometres away, the 24 kilometres on horse-drawn carts, over a muddy, pot-holed, and over-used country road were a nightmare.

Throughout his life, Williams was a hard worker and had excellent business skills, which served him well in the oil industry. He seemed to be lucky, too. Where he bought land, he found oil. Other speculators who set up near him did not. His operation was now a complete business in the sense that he bought the land, he found the oil, he extracted and refined it, and he shipped it, and eventually sold it — all under the original name of J.M. Williams and Co. He later changed the name to The Canadian Oil Co. and appointed himself as president . . . and why not.

He was also the first person in the world to successfully drill for

2 Morrit, p. 32.

oil. He had first attempted to drill at his earlier wells at Bothwell, but he abandoned them when the drill broke. He tried this method again at Oil Springs in 1859, and this time he was successful. The Ruffner Brothers of West Virginia had attempted to find salt in the early 1800s, using a drill. They adapted a method used for centuries by the Chinese. But before Williams, no one had successfully drilled for oil!

The technique was called the "spring pole" method of drilling, and it consisted of a 6 centimetre (2½ inch) steel chisel bit connected to a long iron drill that was alternately raised and dropped by means of a rope or cable that was attached to a "spring pole." This system is still in use today — in a far more sophisticated way — by many water-well drillers.

Why drill? Because it was faster and more efficient, and a drill could bore through rock and other hard layers. (However, Williams' drill was a far cry from the monster drills and floating derricks used in the industry today.) In the early years, when Williams was the major oil producer, he did a large business in the nearby cities, in the United States, and abroad. He was that unique and successful blend of inventor, businessman, and entrepreneur.

In 1858, when he discovered his first oil reserves, he was only 40 years old, but his hair was already steel grey, as were his mustache and bushy side whiskers. He was a handsome man, but he looked much older than his years. He was a deeply religious man and was devoted to his church — which, incidentally, he provided with free oil to keep the church lights burning constantly. He was reliable, dependable, and totally devoted to his family, which remained his major joy throughout his life.

While he was recognized all over the world for his discovery of oil and for his pioneer work in the oil industry, Canada has been slow in recognizing and honouring this man, who anywhere else in the world would be a national icon.

(And yes, he did finally bury the remains of his baby brother in the family plot in Hamilton, Ontario.)

Thomas "Carbide" Willson

Inventor and Pioneer: Acetylene and the Carbide Industry

A failed experiment produced something he neither expected nor could identify immediately . . . but this accidental something eventually brought him great wealth and fame.

I t is sometimes said that it is better to be lucky than to be smart, but it is even better to be *both* if you can manage it! Thomas "Carbide" Willson was both. His intellectual curiosity and energy, coupled with his incredible good luck, brought him wealth and fame in his lifetime, and left a lasting legacy in the discoveries he made, in the inventions he created, and in the industries that his ideas spawned. And some of those industries are even more important today than they were in Willson's own time.

A failed experiment produced something he neither expected nor could identify immediately. But all the luck in the world would not have mattered if his intuition and curiosity had not led him to recognize that this "something" he had created by accident was worth investigating further. The accidental "something" was acetylene, a gas that has become increasingly important in our age of plastics, steel, and modern metals. The other product of this failed experiment was calcium carbide, from which acetylene could be produced inexpensively, and from which Willson acquired his nickname. He was known to everyone (except his mother) as "Carbide" Willson, and he was famous throughout the industrial world for his pioneering work in the chemical industry. But he is largely forgotten today, even in most Canadian textbooks, which make only a passing reference to him and his accomplishments if they acknowledge him at all.

"Carbide" Willson was born Thomas Leopold Willson in 1860, in the small town of Princeton, near Woodstock, in southwestern Ontario. His grandfather was a Baptist minister who also served in the Upper Canada legislature for over a quarter of a century. Willson's father was a farmer, who also tried his hand at a number of other things. His father's sudden death, when Thomas was only 14 years old, put a great economic burden on Thomas's mother, who wanted to do the best she could for her three children. They moved to Hamilton, where his mother not only took in boarders, but also taught music and art in order to provide for her family. She had a profound influence on her children, and Thomas was determined to repay her for all her sacrifices by making her life easier when he grew up. And he did!

In high school at Hamilton Collegiate Institute (which still exists today), he excelled at sciences, and it was clear that he would find his future in the world of science. When Willson left high school, he was apprenticed to blacksmith John Rogers, which gave him the opportunity to work with forges, bellows, metals, and other "white hot" stuff. This apprenticeship was an important foundation for some of Willson's future discoveries. He also was able to do his experiments at the foundry with the support of John Rogers.

One of his first accomplishments was to build a steam-driven dynamo that was wired to an arc lamp, which in turn produced Hamilton's first electric light. Willson patented his version of the electric lighting system when he was only 21 years old. It was the first of over 70 patents he would take out in his lifetime. In his enthusiasm for his lighting system, which was still only at the experimental stage, he entered into contracts with a hotel and a factory to supply them with steady and reliable illumination. His system produced neither, and he lost the contracts. He was also deeply in debt and was forced to move to New York to avoid his creditors and to start over again ... Which he did, only to fail again.

This became the pattern of his life! He had as many failures as successes, and while his successes were brilliant, he was never deterred by his failures.

He was driven not just by his need to invent, but also by the need to develop practical applications for his inventions. The same entrepreneurial spirit that drove other inventors such as Edison, Wright, and Bell also drove Willson. He was fascinated with electricity and its potential application in many new directions. One of these new directions was the development of electric furnaces and forges, which could produce intense heat almost equal to the surface of the sun. The intense heat could then be used to produce new metals and chemicals that were beyond the capabilities of the existing simple technology of the time. One of the new metals was aluminum, which was difficult to make and very expensive.

Willson decided he would find a practical way to produce aluminum with an electric furnace. But he needed a large source of power to heat his furnace, and this was provided by Major James Turner Moorehead of Spray, North Carolina, who owned a water powered cotton mill in Spray and had water power to spare.

Willson built an electric furnace in Spray and established the Willson Aluminum Co. with great expectations of finding a better way to produce aluminum. He was heading down the wrong track again, although he didn't know it. A better way to produce aluminum had already been found. But during his search, Willson had been asked by a customer if he could make him some calcium in his furnace. Willson thought he could. He boiled coal tar and lime together until the mixture was dry. Then he heated the mixture in the intense heat generated by his furnace. The mixture he produced, he presumed was calcium. And if it was calcium, when it was dropped into a container of water, it would bubble and turn the water milky and would produce odourless hydrogen gas as its by-product. Everything worked as Willson predicted, except the gas that was given off had a strange odour like garlic, and when it was lit, it burned with a brilliant white light and produced lots of soot, which hydrogen didn't do. Hydrogen is odourless and burns with a soft blue flame, so the gas was clearly not hydrogen; and therefore the material from the furnace was probably not calcium as Willson had expected. But what was it? Willson set out to find the answer. And that answer made him an extremely wealthy man.

The dark brown solid material he had produced proved to be calcium carbide, and the gaseous by-product that burned with the brilliant white light was acetylene. While Willson was not the first person to discover these compounds, he was the first to be able to make them in commercial quantities at a fraction of the cost of producing them in the lab. In fact, he produced them at one millionth of the cost of the laboratory product and brought them within financial reach of almost everyone.

The first and most obvious use for acetylene was in lamps, where the brilliant white light it produced was vastly more illuminating than the light from Gesner's kerosene or from Edison's electric light (which was not yet readily available in homes, anyway). It was said at the time that "burning acetylene looked like sunshine"[1] when compared to all other light sources.

Carbide Willson did several things after his successful discovery of acetylene. He leased the rights to his patents to many manufacturers, which provided him with a great deal of money. He built his own calcium carbide factory at Merriton, Ontario, near his home in St. Catharines. Both home and factory were situated near an abundance of potential hydro-electric energy generated at Niagara Falls. He also built a mansion for his mother in Woodstock, Ontario, and he sold it to her for $1.00, thus providing for her ease and comfort as he had been determined to do. After a long courtship, he married Mary Parks from California. He eventually sold his patents to Union Carbide, which developed into one of the world's giant corporations of the twentieth century.

In addition to its initial use as a lamp fuel in homes, acetylene was also used for lamps on carriages, automobiles, trains, bicycles, miners' helmets, lighthouses, and street lamps — anywhere that high intensity light was important. But as a gas, it had certain disadvantages. How do you capture, contain, transport, and utilize a gas? Willson experimented with liquefying and solidifying the gas. But a devastating accident in the harbour of Kingston, Ontario, killed four people when a shipping buoy exploded as it was being filled with liquid acetylene. Willson had a new problem to solve and a frightened public that needed to be reassured. He redesigned the buoys! They were now filled with calcium carbide

---

[1]   Michael Webb. *Thomas Willson: Mr. Carbide* (Toronto: Copp Clark Pitman Ltd., 1991), p. 15.

and were fitted with an automatic water feed that allowed the buoys to produce their own acetylene as needed. Another patent . . . another factory where the buoys were built . . . and more income. While everything Willson did at this point seemed to make him richer, he was "not in the inventing business for the profits."[2] When he completed one thing, he became restless to move on to the next.

In the course of his experiments with calcium carbide, he had discovered that hot calcium carbide when exposed to the air took in nitrogen, which in turn produced cyanamide — a fertilizer. This discovery ultimately led to the development of another giant corporation and a new enterprise for him.

By 1911, he had three factories in the Ottawa area, including a commercial power station, a fertilizer factory, and the company that manufactured shipping buoys. He built a summer home at Meech Lake outside Ottawa in order to be close to his operations, and it included a laboratory, so Willson could do more inventing.

While he could have lived the rest of his life in comfort and luxury, it was not in his nature to do so. He again risked his fortune; this time, on developing super phosphate fertilizers. This enterprise failed, and he lost his fortune — again! But he was ever the entrepreneur, and recognizing that the patents he had sold earlier did not include Newfoundland and Labrador (which were not part of Canada at the time), he set out to build new factories there. He had secured British financial backing to proceed in 1914, but World War I intervened, and the British funding was withdrawn. Willson was undeterred. He set off to New York in 1915 to find new backers for his enterprise. He died from a heart attack there on the streets of New York, doing what he — as the entrepreneur — loved to do.

It is an interesting footnote to his vision that the great hydroelectric power plant that he dreamed of for Labrador was finally realized 60 years later when the giant Churchill Falls hydroelectric power plant was opened in 1974 — the largest in the western world.

And what of acetylene? Originally used primarily for lighting,

2 Carole Precious. "Thomas Carbide Willson," *The Canadians: Teachers' Handbook*, Rosalind Sharpe and Roderick Stewart eds. (Toronto: Fitzhenry & Whiteside Ltd., 1983), p. 125.

its uses are far more varied today, and it is even more important in our world of steel, plastic, and concrete. When a French inventor combined acetylene with oxygen to produce the oxyacetylene torch in 1903, it opened new vistas for our modern industrial society, and subsequently changed the skylines of our cities. The oxyacetylene torch can cut through steel like a knife through butter and can weld metal to metal, both of which are key features in our modern automobile industry, our shipbuilding industry, and our construction industry — in fact, in any industry that deals with the cutting and welding of steel and other metals. Acetylene is also used today in the manufacture of vinyl chloride for plastics and for the neoprene type of synthetic rubber.

In addition to developing calcium carbide and acetylene, Willson held patents on electric lights and smelting processes. He produced the first super phosphate fertilizers. He was also a pioneer in the development of newsprint, sulphites, hydro-electric energy, and a whole host of derivative inventions.

Few Canadians remember Willson today. After his death, his Meech Lake property fell into disuse and gradually slid into gentle decay. The property like the man was slowly forgotten by time. Ironically, both the products and industries that were developed from Willson's discoveries are now household words. While it is true that his life was made up of as many failures as successes, his successes were exceptional, and they contributed not only to what we are, but also to how we live. Thomas "Carbide" Willson's major discoveries are even more important today than he could have imagined.

John Joseph Wright

Inventor and Pioneer: Electric Streetcar and the Electrical Industry

Wright had, by his ingenuity, created a growing demand for his electrical power generator, and he consolidated this position by incorporating his operation under the name Toronto Electric Light Company (TELC) in 1883.

Have you ever wondered who turned on the electric lights —for the *first* time?

For today's generation, it is nearly impossible to imagine a world without electricity; without computers, radios, televisions or VCRs, CD players, and night hockey games. Not even electric light bulbs! But just a little over a century ago, none of these existed! Marshall McLuhan seemed to say that in order to understand the miracle of the invention, you must be able to comprehend the world before the invention. So what was life like before electric power?

In 1875, Toronto streets were lit by gas lamps, streetcars were pulled by horses, and the telephone system did not exist. Yet, just ten years later, electric lights illuminated the streets, electric streetcars had been developed, and the first telephone system was in place.

All these inventions were made possible because of the development of a steady and reliable source of electrical energy. The man behind the "power" was John Joseph Wright, electrical pioneer of genius, who was an inventor, an entrepreneur, an innovator, and a man of unique vision.

But just who was John Joseph Wright? You won't find him in many books on inventors or important Canadians, even though his contribution to our modern electrically powered world is significant.

John Joseph Wright was born in 1848, in Yarmouth, England, and obtained a classical education at Shireland Hall in Birmingham. He came to Toronto as a young man and worked briefly at the *Toronto Globe* newspaper as a proofreader. In the mid-1870s he went to Philadelphia and worked with the electrical pioneers Thomson and Houston in developing their coal-fueled electrical generator, which became the standard power source for street lights in many cities. Wright is credited with installing North America's first electric arc street lamp in Philadelphia. As well, he pioneered the concept of placing the electrical wires underground for the street lighting in Market Square in Philadelphia, an idea that was far ahead of its time.

He returned to Toronto permanently in 1879 and began to develop that necessary link between invention, its practical application, and a commercial market for it. While Toronto inventors Henry Woodward and Matthew Evans invented an incandescent electric light bulb in 1874, and received a U.S. patent for their invention, they could not find financial backers to turn it into a practical, commercial venture. Thomas Edison on the other hand, was both an inventor and an entrepreneur. Even though he patented his light bulb (with essentially the same design) five years after Woodward and Evans, he had the financial backing to make it a commercial success.

Wright followed Edison's pattern. When he returned from Philadelphia, he not only brought back the technology to build Canada's first electric generator, he also sold the system of indoor lighting as the product of his generator to some of Toronto's downtown businesses, including Eaton's department store.

Wright established Canada's first commercial generating station, providing power to multiple customers, and its success helped to pave the way for the explosive growth in demand for electrical energy throughout the twentieth century. Practically everything we touch or do today relies to some extent on electrical power.

As an entrepreneur and promoter of electrical energy, Wright took on the contract to light the Canadian Industrial Exhibition in 1882. It was an enormous success, allowing the exhibition grounds to stay open after dark, and lighting up the Toronto skyline. "At least one Toronto clergyman denounced the electric motor as an 'instrument of evil' since it threatened to 'release girls from honest toil to wander the streets and fall prey to the wiles of Satan'."[1]

In 1883, Wright was asked to develop an electric streetcar as a novelty ride for patrons of the exhibition. His streetcar ran on iron tracks and was driven by a third track cogwheel. It covered a distance of one kilometre from Strachan Avenue into the exhibition grounds. It was the first electric streetcar of any kind in Canada, and it gave the exhibition patrons a look at the future of urban transportation.

Toronto, like other growing cities at the time, had a street railway system of horse-drawn carriages that operated along iron tracks. Wright's electric streetcar changed all that! At the 1885 Exhibition, he and his partner Charles Van Depoele introduced a radically new concept to his previous design: an overhead electrical wire as the power source for his trolley car. In this design, the trolley pole that was attached vertically to the trolley car touched the overhead power line and carried electrical power down the trolley pole to the drive mechanism under the car. This concept was to become the general standard streetcar design in most European and North American cities (including Toronto) for most of the next century. Its principle is still used extensively in most urban and inter-city trains in Europe today . It is interesting to note that the first streetcar was "officially" introduced in Richmond, Virginia, in 1887, four years after it had been introduced in Toronto. (Such is the world of invention!)

The first electric streetcar system in Canada was introduced in Windsor, Ontario, in 1886, and in St. Catharines, Ontario, in 1887. Other cities followed suit, including Toronto in 1889. By the early 1890s, horse drawn streetcars had become a thing of the past as a

---

[1] Robert M. Stamp. *Bright Lights; Big City: The History of Electricity in Toronto,* A catalogue published in conjunction with the Exhibition "Bright Lights; Big City" at the Market Gallery of the City of Toronto Archives. (Toronto: 1971), p. 13.

result of Wright's electric streetcar, and a new era of mass urban transportation had begun. Wright had, by his ingenuity, created a growing demand for his electrical power, and he consolidated this position by incorporating his operation underthe name Toronto Electric Light Company (TELC) in 1883.

In expanding the business, he brought in some financial backers, including Sir Henry Pellatt, who is mainly remembered today as the man who built Casa Loma. By the turn of the century, financial control of the company had passed to Pellatt and his associates, and the TELC was now a large private utility. Wright stayed on for the next 25 years as superintendent and then manager and vice-president. However, the private utilities' days were numbered as governments moved in to take control through their own utilities.

Wright remained a man greatly respected in his day for the leadership he gave in developing the electrical systems in Toronto. He was a key player in the electrical movement in both Canada and the United States, serving as one of the founding members of the Canadian Electrical Association. He was also a member of the National Conference of Electricians that was convened by the United States government in 1883 to explore the future of electricity. In addition, he was a member of the Philadelphia Franklin Institute of Science and Arts.

He was a big pleasant man with a shock of unruly hair, sparkling blue eyes, and a large, drooping mustache. He was known to everyone as "J.J." He lived in Parkdale in the west end of Toronto and served on the Parkdale Town Council in 1886.

An historical plaque that is affixed to the wall of the Toronto Hydro building on Carlton Street East in Toronto states that "J.J. Wright introduced electric lighting to Toronto and pioneered the development and use of Canada's first electric street railway. He went on to a distinguished career as vice-president of the Toronto Electric Light Company and in 1891 was the founding president of the Canadian Electrical Association."

It is one of the ironies of our world that people generally do not remember their roots. When I inquired at the Toronto Hydro office, I could not find one person who knew who J.J. Wright was and what he had done, even though they passed a memorial to him every working day. But J.J. Wright was on the front end of the modern wave. He created commercial electricity first, and then set about creating a demand for it with his inventions and innovations. The perfect combination of inventor *and* entrepreneur.

"More than anyone else it was . . . J.J. Wright who introduced Toronto to the wonders of the electric age,"[2] who invented the electric trolley car, who pioneered mass urban transportation, and who turned on the electric lights in Toronto.

[2] Stamp, p. 12.

References

The Atlantic Advocate "Poor John Patch" January 1978.

Bassett, John M. *The Canadians: Samuel Cunard*. Don Mills: Fitzhenry & Whiteside, 1974.

Boulton, Marsha. *Just a Minute*. Toronto: Little, Brown & Company, 1994.

Buchanan, Alison et al. *Canadians All (7) Portraits of Our People*. Toronto: Methuen Publications, 1987.

Canadian Encyclopedia (2nd. Edition) Edmonton: Hurtig Publishers, 1988.

Colapinto, John. "Woman of the Year" *Chatelaine* January 1993.

Coleman, Terry. *The Liners*. Harmondsworth, Middlesex England: Penguin Books Ltd., 1974.

Cruise, David and Alison Griffiths. *Lords of the Line*. Markham: Penguin Books Canada Ltd., 1988.

Dotto, Lydia. *University of Toronto Alumni Magazine* Winter 1996

Earthkeeper Magazine June/July 1993..

Globe and Mail Various articles. Judy Steed, "A Crusader . . . " June 10, 1982; Stephen Strauss, "A Chemist . . ." November 3, 1994; Joanne Strong, "The Informal . . ." August 14, 1982; author unknown) "Professor McLennan . . . " March 31, 1924.

Gridgeman, N.T. *Biological Sciences at the National Research Council of Canada: the Early Years*. Waterloo: Wilfrid Laurier University Press, 1980.

Gross, Renie. *Dinosaur Country*. Saskatoon: Western Producer Prairie Books, 1985.

Hacker, Carlotta. *The Book of Canadians*. Edmonton: Hurtig Publishers, 1983.

Halpenny, Francess, G. *Dictionary of Canadian Biography* Vol. VII 1841–1850; and Vol. XII 1891–1900. Toronto: University of Toronto Press, 1960.

Higham, Charles and Roy Molsey. *Cary Grant: The Lonely Heart*. New York: Harcourt, Brace, Jovanovich, 1989.

Hogg, Helen Sawyer. *The Stars Belong to Everyone* Toronto: Doubleday, 1976.

Inglis, *Northern Vagabond*. Toronto: McClelland & Stewart, 1978.

Imperial Oil Review June/July 1933, February 1946.

Kennedy, Arthur Jr. *The Bermudian* August 1932.

Lamb, W. Kaye. *History of the Canadian Railway.* New York/Toronto: Macmillan Publishing Co. Inc., 1977.

Laycock, Margaret and Barbara Myrvold. *Parkdale in Pictures.* Toronto: Toronto Public Library Board, 1992.

Lesley, Cole. *The Life of Noel Coward.* Harmondsworth, Middlesex, England: Penguin Books Ltd., 1979.

The Liberal Newspaper January 31, 1993.

Marsh, James, ed. *The Junior Encyclopedia of Canada.* Edmonton: Hurtig Publishers, 1990.

McLean, Hugh. *Man of Steel: The Story of Sir Sandford Fleming.* Toronto: The Ryerson Press, 1969.

Merritt, Susan E. *Her Story II: Women from Canada's Past.* St. Catharines: Vanwell Publishing Limited, 1995.

Morrit, Hope. *Rivers of Oil: The Founding of America's Petroleum Industry.* Kingston: Quarry Press, 1993.

The National Aviation Museum. *A Flypast.* Ottawa: National Aviation Museum, 1991.

New York Herald Tribune Obituaries, (Fessenden, Reginald Aubrey), July 22, 1932.

Palmer, David D. *The Palmers: The Memoirs of Daniel D. Palmer.* Davenport (Iowa): Bowden Brothers, 1978.

Parkin, J.H. *Canadian Aeronautical Journal* January/February 1956.

Precious, Carole. "Thomas Carbide Willson" in *The Canadians: Teacher's Handbook* (Sharpe and Stewart, eds.). Toronto: Fitzhenry & Whiteside, 1983.

Rayner-Canham, Marlene F. and Geoffrey W. Rayner-Canham. *Harriet Books: Pioneer Nuclear Scientist.* Montreal/Kingston: McGill-Queen's University Press, 1992.

Ruby, Ormond. *A Short Résumé of the Life of Reginald Fessenden* compiled by Ormond Ruby in Toronto.

The Runic Report July 1971.

Scientific American. "Patch's Propellor" October 1848.

Shaw, Carole P. *Famous Scots.* Glasgow: Harper Collins Publishing, 1995.

Shaw, Margaret Mason. *The Canadians.* Toronto: Fitzhenry & Whiteside, 1976.

Smallie, Dr. Paul. *Encyclopedia Chiropractica.* Stockton (California): World Wide Books Ltd., 1990.

Stamp, Robert M. *Bright Lights; Big City: The History of Electricity in Toronto* in conjunction with the Exhibition "Bright Lights; Big City" at the Market Gallery of Toronto Archives. Toronto, 1971.

Stelco Today "John Patch and the Marine Propeller" July 1990.

Stevenson, William. *A Man Called Intrepid: The Secret War.* New York/London: Harcourt, Brace, Jovanovich, 1976.

Stoichoff, Dr. Boris. *Physics in Canada* Vol. 28, 1972.

Toronto Globe "Canada's Assets . . ." November 24, 1919.

Toronto Star Various articles. "Science Conquers. . ." October 4, 1915; "The Spotlights: McLennan" March 8, 1922; Obituaries, (Burton, Eli Franklin) July 7, 1948, "No Rocking Chair . . . " July 5, 1980.

Toronto Telegram "The Proudest . . ." September 28, 1907.

Wallace, Steward W., ed. *Macmillan Dictionary of Biography.* Toronto: The Macmillan Co. of Canada Ltd., 1978.

Wasson, Tyler. *Nobel Prize Winners.* An H. W. Biographical Dictionary. New York: H.W. Wilson Publishing Co., 1987.

Waterston, Elizabeth. *Pioneers in Agriculture.* Toronto: Clarke, Irwin and Company, 1957.

Webb, Michael. *Thomas Willson: Mr. Carbide.* Toronto: Copp Clark Pitman, 1991.

Woodcock, George. *Faces from History.* Edmonton: Hurtig Publishers, 1978.

Yarmouth County Museum Archives. Various articles.

Index